LESESTOFF NACH WAHL

EINFÜHRUNG

LESESTOFF NACH WAHL

EINFÜHRUNG

URSULA THOMAS
with the cooperation of Freeman Twaddell

THE UNIVERSITY OF WISCONSIN PRESS

Published 1977
The University of Wisconsin Press
Box 1379, Madison, Wisconsin 53701

The University of Wisconsin Press, Ltd.
70 Great Russell Street, London

First printing

Printed in the United States of America

LC 76-11321
ISBN 0-299-07144-8

Acknowledgment is made to the following for permission to use copyrighted
material: for "Was ist Nylon?" and "Chlor" from WIE, WAS, WARUM, published by Neuer Tessloff Verlag, Hamburg, Copyright © 1968, from TELL
ME WHY by Arkady Leokum, Copyright © 1965 by Arkady Leokum; used by per-
mission of Grosset & Dunlap, Inc.; for "Ich bin Schweizer," entnommen aus
Peter Bichsel "Des Schweizers Schweiz", Copyright (C) 1969 by Verlags AG
"Die Arche", Peter Schifferli, Zürich; and for "Fondue oder Der Freitisch,"
aus Hans Bender "Worte Bilder Menschen" C 1969 Carl Hanser Verlag, München.
"Was Säugetiere fressen," "Das Gebiß der Pflanzenfresser," "Das Gebiß der
Fleischfresser," and "Das Gebiß der Allesfresser" are from Biologie von
Tieren und Pflanzen, Ein Lehrbuch für die 5. Klasse, Volk und Wissen
Volkseigener Verlag, Berlin, 1966.

To the hundreds of students whose
suggestions and criticisms over
the years have contributed to the
development of these materials.

Contents

Literatur

This book, Lesestoff nach Wahl: Einführung, is the first part of the learning materials for a total course. It is for use at the beginning of the semester, followed by one of four Collections representing several major styles of written German, to be selected by you: (1) the Physical Sciences, (2) the Social Studies, (3) the Life Sciences, (4) Imaginative Literature. This "Einführung" is a review and refresher of your knowledge of German from previous study, both vocabulary and the important principles of German grammar.

The readings were not chosen primarily for the information they present, but for their usefulness in your language learning. Your increasing confidence in your understanding of German and in your ability to express yourself are the pleasures you can expect to get out of this course. The overriding aim of the materials is to give you some essential skills and resources, to enable you to sit down, if necessary with a dictionary, and read what you need or consider interesting, with confidence and with pleasure.

The structure of the reading units:

The first reading unit is general and unspecialized in nature. The four remaining units are simple examples of each of the four major styles of written German which will be studied in the specialized Collections.

Each section of a reading unit is a segment-by-segment presentation of a German text and its English rendering, in parallel columns. Following the text are some "Notes on Language" and "Words and Word Families." The latter lists various vocabulary items to be learned by heart.

Each section next presents "Comments on Grammar," a thumbnail sketch of one or two grammatical topics.

A tear-out exercise sheet provides practice of the grammar of the section.

The last of the reading units — a sample of imaginative literature — anticipates the format of the units of the specialized Collections. It presents the parallel-column arrangement at the beginning of the story, followed by the entire text without English renderings, but with a full set of line-by-line footnotes, and content questions in English and German.

The Grammar Reference Notes:

These are midway between the presentation of grammar in an elementary German course and a complete, detailed grammar of German. There are frequent cross-references to the Grammar Reference Notes both in this "Einführung" and in each of the specialized Collections. Since the Notes are not reprinted in the Collections, you must keep this book available during the entire course.

The specialized Collections:

    You have your choice among four specialized Collections.
Each of these consists of nine Units. The contents of each
Collection:

Physik und Chemie

1   Das perpetuum mobile
2   Die chemische Zeichensprache
3   Zur Geschichte der Atommodelle
4   Das mechanische Wärmeäquivalent
5   Das Bohrsche Atommodell
6   Das Quecksilberbarometer
     Die elektrische Entladung in Gasen
7   Die Elektronenstrahlen
8   Kohlenstoffverbindungen
9   Polymerisation

*[The selections offered here are meant to prepare you to read
materials in the physical sciences. The readings have been
taken from elementary textbooks and are relatively simple as
science, but you should not choose this option unless you have
had at least a year of college chemistry and/or physics, or a
good high-school course.]*

Mensch und Gesellschaft

1   Fernseh-Interview
2   Nachbarn, die bekannten Unbekannten
3   „Die Frau gilt im Beruf wenig"
     Industrie und Wirtschaft der DDR
4   Emigration und Widerstand: Emigration
5   Emigration und Widerstand: Widerstand
6   Das Stimm- und Wahlrecht in der Schweiz
7   „Wer ist ein guter Deutscher?"
8   Die Fundamente der österreichischen Demokratie
9   Österreich: Geographie und Bevölkerung

*[The selections in this group of readings cover a variety of topics
of an economic, sociological, and political nature. They prepare
you to read German newspapers and articles in journals dealing
with the social studies. These will best serve the person who has
done a good deal of reading of newspapers and journals on his own.]*

Biologie

1   Die Bedeutung der Zellenlehre
2   Familie Kieferngewächse
3   Organismen und ihre Umwelt
4   Gesetzmäßigkeiten der Vererbung
5   Die Mendelschen Gesetze: Fortsetzung
6   Für viele ist Milch ungesund
7   Beziehungen zwischen den Pflanzen einer
       Lebensgemeinschaft
    Beziehungen zwischen Pflanzen und Tieren
       innerhalb von Biozönosen
8   Biozönotisches Gleichgewicht
9   Das Wesen des Lebens

[These selections have been taken mainly from textbooks on biology used in German schools. Although the readings are not highly technical, you should not choose this option unless you have had at least a good high-school course in biology.]

Literatur

1   Der Hefekuchen (Kusenberg)
    Heidenröslein (Goethe)
    Der König in Thule (Goethe)
2   Das Fenster-Theater (Aichinger)
    Die Wallfahrt nach Kevlaar (Heine)
3   Bekenntnis eines Hundefängers (Böll)
    Drei Liebesgedichte (Heine)
4   Kinder sind immer Erben (von der Grün)
    Der Zauberlehrling (Goethe)
5   Ein Bild von Mann und Frau (Eisenreich)
    Das zerbrochene Ringlein (Eichendorff)
    Mondnacht (Eichendorff)
6   Der Gattungsstil (Kerkhoff)
    Nachtgeräusche (C. F. Meyer)
7   Die Entscheidung (von der Grün)
    Die Erblindende (Rilke)
8   Die dreifache Warnung (Schnitzler)
    Der 23. Psalm (aus der Bibel)
    Der verlorene Sohn (aus der Bibel)
9   Die Weise von Liebe und Tod des Cornets
       Christoph Rilke (Rilke)
    Wandrers Nachtlied (Goethe)

[The readings in this group prepare you to read fiction and poetry of the 19th and 20th centuries. The prose selections come from the 20th century, and the poetry mainly from the 19th. There is one discussion of style, and two short passages from the Bible.]

EINFÜHRUNG

RUMPELSTILZCHEN

       Es war einmal
ein Müller,
der war arm,
aber er hatte
5 eine schöne Tochter.
Nun traf es sich,
daß er mit dem König zu sprechen
       kam,
und um sich ein Ansehen zu geben,

sagte er zu ihm:
10 „Ich habe eine Tochter,
die kann Stroh zu Gold spinnen."
Der König sagte zum Müller:
„Das ist eine Kunst,
die mir wohl gefällt;
15 wenn deine Tochter so geschickt
       ist,
wie du sagst,
so bring sie morgen in mein Schloß,
da will ich sie auf die Probe
       stellen.
Als nun das Mädchen zu ihm ge-
       bracht wurde,
20 führte er es in eine Kammer,
die ganz voll Stroh lag,
gab ihr Rad und Haspel
und sagte:
„Jetzt mache dich an die Arbeit,
25 und wenn du
bis morgen früh
dieses Stroh nicht zu Gold ver-
       sponnen hast,
so mußt du sterben."
Darauf schloß er die Kammer selbst
       zu,
30 und sie blieb allein darin.
       Da saß nun die arme
Müllerstochter

und wußte um ihr Leben keinen Rat:

sie verstand gar nichts davon,

35 wie man Stroh zu Gold spinnen
       konnte,

und ihre Angst wurde immer größer,

bis sie endlich zu weinen anfing.
Da ging auf einmal die Tür auf,
ein kleines Männchen trat herein
40 und sagte:
„Guten Abend, Jungfer Müllerin,
warum weint sie so sehr?"
„Ach," antwortete das Mädchen,

„ich soll Stroh zu Gold spinnen

RUMPELSTILTSKIN

   Once upon a time there was
a miller;
he was poor,
but he had
a beautiful daughter.
Now it happened

that he was speaking to the king,
and in order to give himself stand-
       ing,
he said to him,
"I have a daughter,
and she can spin straw into gold."
The king said to the miller,
"That is an art
that I like very much;

if your daughter is as clever

as you say,
bring her to my castle tomorrow;

I want to put her to the test.

When the girl was brought to him,

he led her to a chamber
which was completely full of straw,
gave her a (spinning) wheel and reel,
and said,
"Now start working,
and if you,
by tomorrow morning,

haven't spun this straw into gold,

you will have to die."
Thereupon he locked the chamber him-
       self,
and she remained alone inside.
   Well, there sat the poor
miller's-daughter
and for the life of her didn't know
       what to do:
she didn't understanding anything
       at all about
how a person could spin straw into
       gold,
and her anxiety became greater and
       greater
until she finally began to cry.
Then all of a sudden the door opened,
a tiny little man entered
and said,
"Good evening, miller maiden,
why are you crying so much?"
"Oh," answered the girl,
"I am supposed to spin straw into
       gold

3

45 und verstehe das nicht."	and don't understand how."
Das Männchen sagte:	The little man said,
„Was gibst du mir,	"What will you give me
wenn ich's dir spinne?"	if I spin it for you?"
„Mein Halsband," sagte das Mädchen.	"My necklace," said the girl.
50 Das Männchen nahm das Halsband,	The little man took the necklace,
	sat down in front of the little
	wheel:
setzte sich vor das Rädchen,	
und schnurr, schnurr, schnurr,	
dreimal gezogen,	three pulls, whir, whir, whir,
war die Spule voll.	
Dann steckte es eine andere auf,	and the reel was full.
	Then he put on another:
55 und schnurr, schnurr, schnurr,	
dreimal gezogen,	three pulls, whir, whir, whir,
war auch die zweite voll;	
und so ging's fort bis zum Morgen,	and the second, too, was full;
da war alles Stroh versponnen,	and so it went on until morning;
und alle Spulen waren voll Gold.	then all the straw was spun,
	and all the reels were full of gold.

NOTES ON LANGUAGE

9 sagte er zu ihm: *Direct quotations in German are preceded by a colon.*

10 „Ich habe..." *The quotation marks in German are usually lowered to mark the beginning of the quote.*

12 zum = zu dem

41 Jungfer: *archaic form of address to an unmarried woman*

42 sie: *formerly used as a pronoun of address, "you," intermediate between* Sie *and* du.

48 ich's = ich es

57 ging's = ging es

Note also

19 Mädchen - 20 es;

50 Männchen - 54 es:
The triumph of grammatical gender over biology.

WORDS AND WORD FAMILIES

bringen [§6.1.2] (17, 19)
geben [4a] (8, 22, 47)
morgen (17, 26)
der Müller - (2, 12)

das Rad/Räder (22)
   das Rädchen - (51)
verstehen [§6.2.2] (34, 45)
weinen (37, 42)

Note: Numbers in square brackets refer to the Grammar Reference Notes. Thus bringen [§6.1.2] *means that the principal parts are:* bringen, brachte, gebracht; geben [4a] *means that this verb belongs to one of the classes of strong verbs under* §6.2.1. *The lack of notation after* weinen *indicates that this is a regular weak verb:* weinen, weinte, geweint.

The nouns are listed with their genders and plurals. Examples: der Müller - = der Müller/die Müller; das Jahr -e = das Jahr/die Jahre; das Rad/Räder = das Rad/die Räder. *The numbers in parentheses after each item indicate the segments where occurrences of the item are to be found.*

COMMENTS ON GRAMMAR

Main (independent) clauses and subordinate (dependent) clauses:

The two basic ingredients of a clause are a subject and an
inflected verb. The inflected verb is the form of the verb that
has an ending which agrees with the subject.

The simplest form of a German sentence is a grammatically
independent clause:

> Annemarie lacht.
> Der König sprach.

Usually the main clause contains some elements besides the
subject and the inflected verb:

> Der Müller hatte eine schöne Tochter.
> Die Müllerstochter blieb allein in der Kammer.
> Alle Spulen waren voll Gold.

A main clause may be either a statement (like the examples
above) or a question:

> Ist der Müller arm?
> Kann die Müllerstochter Stroh zu Gold spinnen?
> Warum weinst du so sehr?

Another form of main clause is the imperative, which in the
du-form has no subject:

> Mache dich an die Arbeit!   (Machen Sie sich an die Arbeit!)
> Bring sie morgen in mein Schloß! (Bringen Sie sie morgen ...)

In a main clause the inflected verb is the second element.
(Examine the sentence segments indicated in the left margin.)

10,12,13   In these clauses the first element is a noun or pro-
            noun, the subject of the sentence.

6,18,29   The first element is an adverb: **nun, da, darauf;** and
            each is followed by the verb. Then comes the subject.
            This pattern is in contrast to English:

> Darauf schloß er ... zu *(Thereupon he locked...)*

Two main clauses may be joined by a coordinating conjunction,
like **und, aber, oder, denn.** A coordinating conjunction does not
affect the word order in the clause which follows it.

4,30,36   The order is: coordinating conjunction - first element
            - inflected verb.

33,45   Often the conjunction **und** is used to join two verbs
            with the same subject. In this usage, **und** is followed
            directly by the verb.

A <u>subordinate clause</u> is one which is grammatically incomplete:

> daß er mit dem König zu sprechen kam
> wenn deine Tochter so geschickt ist

A subordinate clause is connected with its main clause by:
(1) a <u>subordinating conjunction</u>, or (2) a <u>relative pronoun</u>.

In a subordinate clause the inflected verb is at the <u>end</u>.

7,15,16,19   These are all subordinate clauses introduced by sub-
             ordinating conjunctions: **daß, wenn, wie, als.** Locate
             the inflected verb in each of these clauses.

14,21   Each of these clauses is introduced by the relative
             pronoun **die.** In 14, **die** refers to **eine Kunst**; in 21,
             die refers to **eine Kammer.** Locate the inflected verb.

<u>Subordinate clauses</u> are always set off by <u>commas</u>.

Often a sentence begins with a subordinate clause. Then this
clause is the first element of the complete sentence, and the
verb of the main clause immediately follows it.

Analysis of the sentence which runs through segments 19-23:

19   A subordinate clause with a subordinating conjunction.
20   Verb of the main clause, followed by the subject **er**
     and the rest of that clause.
21   A relative clause dependent on the noun **Kammer.**
22   A second verb in the main clause, with the subject **er**
     in segment 20.
23   The third verb in the main clause.

Any element of the sentence — the subject, an adverb, the
direct object, the indirect object, a prepositional phrase,
a subordinate clause, for example — may begin a sentence,
always followed by the inflected verb of the main clause.

8   The element **um...zu** + infinitive begins this main
     clause.

In a sentence beginning with a wenn-clause, the verb of the
main clause is often preceded by one of the two adverbs: **so** or
dann.

15-17   wenn...ist, wie...sagst, so bring...
25-28   wenn...hast, so mußt...

Name _____   Datum _____

Examine the clause in each of the following segments and
1) indicate whether it is a main clause or a subordinate clause;
2) copy out the subject and the inflected verb of each clause.
(The first is done as an example.)

	Main/subordinate	Subject	Inflected verb
6	Main	es	traf
7			
8-9			
12			
13			
14			
19			
20			
21			
22			
25-27			
28			
34			
35			
36			
37			
54			
57			
58			
59			

Bei Sonnenaufgang
kam schon der König,
und als er das Gold erblickte,
erstaunte er und freute sich,
5 aber sein Herz
wurde nur noch goldgieriger.
Er ließ die Müllerstochter in eine
    andere Kammer voll Stroh
    bringen,
die noch viel größer war,
und befahl ihr,
10 das auch in einer Nacht zu spinnen,
wenn ihr das Leben lieb wäre.
Das Mädchen wußte sich nicht zu
    helfen
und weinte,
da ging abermals die Tür auf,
15 und das kleine Männchen erschien
und sagte:
„Was gibst du mir, wenn ich dir
    das Stroh zu Gold spinne?"
„Meinen Ring von dem Finger,"
antwortete das Mädchen.
20 Das Männchen nahm den Ring,
fing wieder an zu schnurren mit
    dem Rade
und hatte bis zum Morgen alles
    Stroh zu glänzendem Gold ge-
    sponnen.
Der König freute sich über die
    Maßen bei dem Anblick,
war aber noch immer nicht Goldes
    satt,
25 sondern ließ die Müllerstochter in
    eine noch größere Kammer voll
    Stroh bringen
und sagte:
„Die mußt du noch in dieser Nacht
    verspinnen:
gelingt es dir aber,
so sollst du meine Gemahlin werden."
30 „Wenn's auch eine Müllerstochter
    ist,"
dachte er,
„eine reichere Frau finde ich in
    der ganzen Welt nicht."
Als das Mädchen allein war,
kam das Männlein zum drittenmal
    wieder
35 und sagte:
„Was gibst du mir,
wenn ich dir noch diesmal das Stroh
    spinne?"
„Ich habe nichts mehr,
das ich geben könnte,"
40 antwortete das Mädchen.
„So versprich mir,

At sunup
the king came,
and when he caught sight of the gold
he was astonished and happy,
but his heart
just became still greedier for gold.
He had the miller's daughter brought
    into another chamber full of
    straw,
which was much bigger;
and (he) ordered her
to spin that, too, in one night,
if her life was dear to her.

The girl didn't know what to do

and wept;
then the door opened once again
and the tiny little man appeared
 and said,
 "What will you give me if I spin the
    straw into gold for you?"
 "The ring from my finger,"
answered the girl.
The little man took the ring,

again began to whir with the wheel,

and by morning had spun all the straw
    into gleaming gold.

The king was excessively happy at
    the sight,
still, however, didn't have enough
    gold,
but had the miller's daughter brought
    to a still bigger chamber full
    of straw
and said,

"This you still have to spin tonight:

if you succeed, however,
you are to become my wife."
"Even if it is just a miller's
    daughter,"
he thought,
"I won't find a richer wife in the
    whole world."
When the girl was alone,
the little man came again for the
    third time
and said,
"What will you give me
if I spin the straw for you this
    time?"
"I have nothing else
that I could give,"
answered the girl.
"Well, promise me,

wenn du Königin wirst,   when you become queen,
dein erstes Kind."   your first child."
„Wer weiß, wie das noch geht,"   "Who knows how that will go,"
45 dachte die Müllerstochter   thought the miller's daughter,
und wußte sich auch in der Not   and besides, in her dire need she
    nicht anders zu helfen;   didn't know what else to do.
sie versprach also dem Männlein,   she therefore promised the little man
was es verlangte,   what he demanded,
und das Männchen spann dafür noch   and in return the little man again
    einmal das Stroh zu Gold.   spun the straw into gold.
50 Und als am Morgen der König kam   And when the king came in the morning
und alles fand,   and found everything
wie er es gewünscht hatte,   as he had wished it,
so hielt er Hochzeit mit ihr   he celebrated his wedding with her,
und die schöne Müllerstochter   and the beautiful miller's daughter
55 wurde eine Königin.   became a queen.

NOTES ON LANGUAGE

27 **Die:** die noch größere Kammer voll
Stroh
28 **gelingt es dir aber** = wenn es dir
aber gelingt

*Prepositions cause great difficulty
in translation, because they are
highly idiomatic. Examples:*

  bei Sonnenaufgang – *at sunup*
  Stroh zu Gold – *straw into gold*
  bei dem Anblick – *at the sight*
  am Morgen – *in the morning*
  bis morgen früh – *by tomorrow
      morning*
  um ihr Leben – *for the life of her*

*Note that with a continuing action,
bis is translated "until;" with a
time-goal, it is translated "by."*

WORDS AND WORD FAMILIES

an·fangen [7b] (21)   nehmen [5c] (20)
auf·gehen [§6.2.2] (14)   das Rad/Räder (21)
denken [§6.1.2] (31, 45)   versprechen [5a] (41, 47)
finden [3a] (32, 51)   werden [§6.2.2] (6, 29, 55)
sich freuen (4, 23)   wissen [§6.1.2]:
lassen [7a] + infinitive (7, 25)   sich zu helfen wissen (12, 46)

*Verbs with separable components
[§9.5.1] are indicated by a raised
period: an·fangen. Prefixed verbs
[§9.5.2] are written as a single
string of letters: versprechen.*

COMMENTS ON GRAMMAR

Present-tense verb forms:

    The present tense of a German verb is based on the infinitive stem: **gehen, sammeln, antworten.** (See §6 of the Grammar Reference Notes.)

    The infinitive <u>stem</u> is the infinitive minus the ending **-en/-n:** **geh-, sammel-/samml-, antwort-.**

    The present-tense forms agree with the subject in person (1st, 2nd, 3rd) and number (singular, plural). The endings are:

	Singular	Plural
1st	-e	-en (-n)
2nd	-st (-est)	-t (-et)
3rd	-t (et)	-en (-n)

Examples:

Singular

    (ich) gehe, sammle, antworte
    (du) gehst, sammelst, antwortest
    (er/sie/es or any singular noun) geht, sammelt, antwortet

Plural

    (wir) gehen, sammeln, antworten
    (ihr) geht, sammelt, antwortet
    (sie/Sie or any plural noun) gehen, sammeln, antworten

    Some verbs have a different vowel in the 2nd and 3rd singular from the one in the infinitive stem. (See §6.2.1 of the Grammar Reference Notes.) Examples:

    gefallen: Es gefällt mir.
    geben: Was gibst du mir?

Past-tense verb forms:

    The past tense of a German verb is based on a special past-tense stem, shown in the "past-tense" column of the principal parts in §6. The endings are:

	Singular	Plural
1st	—	-en (-n)
2nd	-st (-est)	-t (-et)
3rd	—	-en (-n)

Examples:

Singular

    (ich) ging, sammelte, antwortete
    (du) gingst, sammeltest, antwortetest
    (er/sie/es or any singular noun) ging, sammelte, antwortete

Plural

    (wir) gingen, sammelten, antworteten
    (ihr) gingt, sammeltet, antwortetet
    (Sie/Sie or any plural noun) gingen, sammelten, antworteten

<u>Irregular tense forms</u>:

   Some verbs have irregularities in the present and past tense forms. Some of the most important ones are:

<u>The auxiliary verbs</u>:

sein

bin	sind
bist	seid
ist	sind

Past stem: war

haben

habe	haben
hast	habt
hat	haben

Past stem: hatte

werden

werde	werden
wirst	werdet
wird	werden

Past stem: wurde

<u>The modal auxiliary verbs</u>:

dürfen

darf	dürfen
darfst	dürft
darf	dürfen

Past stem: durfte

können

kann	können
kannst	könnt
kann	können

Past stem: konnte

mögen

mag	mögen
magst	mögt
mag	mögen

Past stem: mochte

müssen

muß	müssen
mußt	müßt
muß	müssen

Past stem: mußte

sollen

soll	sollen
sollst	sollt
soll	sollen

Past stem: sollte

wollen

will	wollen
willst	wollt
will	wollen

Past stem: wollte

<u>The very irregular verb</u>:

wissen

weiß	wissen
weißt	wißt
weiß	wissen

Past stem: wußte

Name _____   Datum _____

Rewrite the following 20 sentences in the present tense. For
each group of sentences there is a Grammar Reference Note.
[§6.1.1]

  1 Das Mädchen weinte. _____ Das Mädchen weint. _____

  2 „Ach", antwortete das Mädchen.

  ----

  3 Der König erstaunte und freute sich.

[§6.1.2]

  4 Sie wußte keinen Rat.

  ----

  5 „Wer kommt?" dachte ich.

[§6.2.1...]

  6 Sie blieb allein darin. [1a]

  ----

  7 Der König schloß die Kammer selbst zu. [2a]

  ----

  8 Er fand die Kammer voll Gold. [3a]

  ----

  9 Der König gab ihr Rad und Haspel. [4a]

  ----

 10 Die Kammer lag voll Stroh. [4c]

  ----

 11 Da saß nun die arme Müllerstochter. [4d]

  ----

 12 Nun traf es sich,... [5a]

  ----

 13 Der König sprach zum Müller. [5a]

  ----

14 Diese Kunst gefiel dem König wohl. [7a]

----

15 Sie fing zu weinen an. [7b]

[§6.2.2]
16 Da ging auf einmal die Tür auf.

----

17 Der Müller war arm.

----

18 Alle Spulen waren voll Gold.

----

19 Sie verstand nichts davon.

----

20 Ihre Angst wurde immer größer.

Rewrite the following sentences in the past.
[§6.1.3]
 1 Die Königin muß sterben.

----

 2 Sie will nicht sterben.

----

 3 Die Müllerstochter soll Stroh zu Gold spinnen.

----

 4 Man kann nicht Stroh zu Gold spinnen.

Nach einem Jahr	*After a year*
brachte sie ein schönes Kind zur Welt	*she brought a beautiful child into the world*
und dachte gar nicht mehr	*and no longer thought at all*
an das Männchen:	*about the little man;*
5 da trat es plötzlich	*then suddenly he stepped*
in ihre Kammer und sprach:	*into her chamber and spoke:*
„Nun gib mir,	*"Now give me*
was du versprochen hast."	*what you promised."*
Die Königin erschrak	*The queen was frightened*
10 und bot dem Männchen alle Reichtümer des Königsreichs an,	*and offered the little man all the riches of the kingdom*
wenn es ihr das Kind lassen wollte,	*if he would leave her her child;*
aber das Männchen sagte:	*but the little man said,*
„Nein, etwas Lebendes	*"No, something living*
ist mir lieber	*is dearer to me*
15 als alle Schätze der Welt."	*than all the treasures in the world."*
Da fing die Königin so an zu jammern und zu weinen,	*Then the queen began to moan and weep so much*
daß das Männchen Mitleid mit ihr hatte:	*that the little man had sympathy with her:*
„Drei Tage will ich dir Zeit lassen,"	*"I will leave you three days' time,"*
20 sagte er;	*said he;*
„wenn du bis dahin meinen Namen weißt,	*"if by that time you know my name,*
so sollst du dein Kind behalten."	*you are to keep your child."*
Nun besann sich die Königin	*Now the queen racked her brain*
die ganze Nacht über	*the whole night through*
auf alle Namen,	*for all the names*
25 die sie jemals gehört hatte,	*that she had ever heard,*
und schickte einen Boten	*and sent a messenger*
über Land,	*across the land;*
der sollte sich erkundigen	*he was to inquire*
weit und breit,	*far and wide*
30 was es sonst noch für Namen gäbe.	*what other kinds of names there might be.*
Als am andern Tag	*When the next day*
das Männchen kam,	*the little man came*
fing sie an mit Kaspar, Melchior, Balzer,	*she began with Caspar, Melchior, Balthasar,*
und sagte alle Namen,	*and said all the names*
35 die sie wußte,	*that she knew,*
nach der Reihe her,	*one after the other,*
aber bei jedem	*but at each one*
sagte das Männlein:	*the little man said,*
„So heiß' ich nicht."	*"That's not my name."*
40 Den zweiten Tag	*The second day*
ließ sie in der Nachbarschaft herumfragen,	*she had inquiries made in the neighborhood*
wie die Leute da genannt würden,	*as to what names the people there might have,*
und sagte dem Männlein die ungewöhnlichsten und seltsamsten Namen vor:	*and recited to the little man the most unusual, strangest names:*

„Heißt du vielleicht Rippenbiest
        oder Hammelswade oder Schnür-
        bein?"
45 Aber es antwortete immer:
    „So heiß' ich nicht."

"Is your name perhaps Rib-beast, or
        Mutton-leg, or String-leg?"

But he always answered,
"That's not my name."

NOTES ON LANGUAGE

13 etwas Lebendes [§5.5.2]
30 was...für = was für - *what kind
of*: *The two words of the idiom
can be either together or separated.*

Prepositions:

denken (an + *acc.*) - *think of*
nach der Reihe her - *in a row,
    one after another*
bei jedem - *in the case of each
    one*
am andern Tag = am nächsten Tag -
    the next day

The verb lassen:

As an independent verb:

11 wenn es ihr das Kind lassen wollte
    - *if he would leave her the child*
18 drei Tage will ich dir lassen -
    I'll let you have three days

As an auxiliary + infinitive:

41 sie ließ...herumfragen - *she had
    inquiries made...*

Also:
er ließ das Mädchen...bringen -
he had the girl brought...

WORDS AND WORD FAMILIES

heißen [7d] (39, 44, 46)
das Kind -er (2, 11, 21)
der König -e
    die Königin -nen (9)
    das Königsreich -e (10)
lassen [7a] (11, 18)

der Name -n (20, 24, 30, 34)
sollen [§6.1.3] (21, 28)
treten [4a] (5)
sprechen [5a] (6)
    versprechen (8)
der Tag -e (18, 31, 40)

COMMENTS ON GRAMMAR

The perfect verb phrase:

There is a "perfect verb phrase" which is used in talking about the past. It is used in conversations, in contrast with the past tense verb, which is chiefly used to tell a story in formal narrative form.

The perfect verb phrase consists of an inflected form of an auxiliary verb, **haben** or **sein**, + the past participle of the main verb. (The main verb is the verb which carries the burden of meaning. In the present and past tenses it is inflected, in the perfect verb phrase it is the past participle, in the future verb phrase it is the infinitive.)

In a main clause, the inflected form of the auxiliary is the second element; in a subordinate clause the inflected auxiliary is at the end. The past participle occurs at or near the end of the clause.

Most perfect verb phrases have the auxiliary **haben**. The following examples give pairs of sentences: the first with a past-tense verb, the second with a perfect verb phrase.

Past tense	*Perfect verb phrase*
Das Männlein sprach.	Das Männlein hat gesprochen.
Er hatte Mitleid mit ihr.	Er hat Mitleid mit ihr gehabt.
Die Königin besann sich.	Die Königin hat sich besonnen.
Sie schickte Boten über Land.	Sie hat Boten über Land geschickt.
Sie hörte viele Namen.	Sie hat viele Namen gehört.
Das Männlein antwortete immer:	Das Männlein hat immer geantwortet:
„So heiß' ich nicht."	„So heiß' ich nicht."

The auxiliary **sein** is used in perfect verb phrases where
1) there is no accusative object of the verb, and
2) a change of location or condition is expressed.

In addition **sein** and **bleiben** form the perfect verb phrase with **sein**.

Das Männlein trat herein.	Das Männlein ist hereingetreten.
Es kam am andern Tag.	Es ist am andern Tag gekommen.
Boten fuhren weit und breit.	Boten sind weit und breit gefahren.
Auf einmal ging die Tür auf.	Auf einmal ist die Tür aufgegangen.
Das Männchen starb.	Das Männchen ist gestorben.
Der König wurde reich.	Der König ist reich geworden.

The future verb phrase:

In German, as in English, the present tense is often used to express future meaning:

Eine reichere Frau finde ich in der ganzen Welt nicht. *(I won't find a richer wife in the whole world.)*

German has a special future verb phrase which is used for clarity or emphasis to tell about something in the future.

The future verb phrase consists of a present-tense form of the auxiliary verb **werden** + the infinitive of the main verb. In a main clause, the inflected form of the auxiliary is the second element; in a subordinate clause the inflected auxiliary is at the end. The infinitive stands at or near the end of the clause.

   The following examples give pairs of sentences: the first
with a present-tense verb, the second with the future verb
phrase.

Present tense	*Future verb phrase*
Das Männlein spricht.	Das Männlein wird sprechen.
Wir haben Mitleid mit ihr.	Wir werden Mitleid mit ihr haben.
Das Männlein tritt herein.	Das Männlein wird hereintreten.
Ich komme morgen.	Ich werde morgen kommen.
Sie schickt Boten über Land.	Sie wird Boten über Land schicken.
Boten fahren weit und breit.	Boten werden weit und breit fahren.
Der König wacht früh auf.	Der König wird früh aufwachen.
Das Männchen stirbt.	Das Männchen wird sterben.

Name _____   Datum _____

Rewrite the following sentences, changing the past-tense verb
to a perfect verb phrase.   *(First of two exercises.)*

1 Das Männchen trat herein.____ Das Männchen ist hereingetreten.____

2 Ich dachte nicht mehr an das Kind.

----

3 Die Königin brachte ein Kind zur Welt.

----

4 Der König führte das Mädchen in die Kammer.

----

5 Darauf schloß er die Tür zu. [2a]

----

6 Am Ende starb das Männchen. [5a]

----

7 Wir boten ihm alles an. [2a]

----

8 Die Kinder fingen zu weinen an. [7b]

----

9 Die Müllerstochter wurde Königin.

----

10 Wir erkundigten uns weit und breit.

----

11 Sie sagte dem Männlein alle Namen vor.

----

12 Der König und die Königin behielten ihr Kind. [7a]

----

13 Ich blieb allein im Zimmer. [1a]

----

14 Rumpelstilzchen sprach wenig. [5a]

Rewrite the following sentences, changing the present-tense verb
to the future verb phrase.

1 Wir lassen Ihnen drei Tage Zeit.

                    Wir werden Ihnen drei Tage Zeit lassen.
----

2 Ich weiß mir zu helfen.

----

3 Das Mädchen versteht nichts davon.

----

4 Das Männchen nimmt das Halsband.

----

5 Das Kind jammert und weint.

----

6 Die Müllerstochter wird Königin.

Review:

Examine the clause in each of the following segments and
1) indicate whether it is a main clause or a subordinate clause;
2) copy out the subject and the inflected verb of each clause.

	Main/subordinate	Subject	Inflected verb
22-24			
25			
26-27			
28-29			
30			

Den dritten Tag
kam der Bote wieder zurück
und erzählte:
„Neue Namen habe ich keinen ein-
　　zigen finden können,
5 aber wie ich an einen hohen Berg
　　um die Waldecke kam,
wo Fuchs und Hase sich gute Nacht
　　sagen,
so sah ich da ein kleines Haus,
und vor dem Haus brannte ein
　　Feuer,
und um das Feuer sprang
10 ein gar zu lächerliches Männchen,

hüpfte auf einem Bein
und schrie:
‚Heute back' ich, morgen brau' ich,
übermorgen hol' ich der Königin
　　ihr Kind;
15 ach, wie gut es ist, daß niemand
　　weiß,
daß ich Rumpelstilzchen heiß'.'"
　　Da könnt ihr denken,
wie die Königin froh war,
als sie den Namen hörte,
20 und als bald hernach
das Männchen hereintrat
und fragte:
„Nun, Frau Königin, wie heiß'
　　ich?"
fragte sie erst:
25 „Heißt du Kunz?" — „Nein."
„Heißt du Heinz?" — „Nein."
„Heißt du etwa Rumpelstilzchen?"
„Das hat dir der Teufel gesagt,
das hat dir der Teufel gesagt,"
30 schrie das Männlein
und stieß mit dem rechten Fuß
vor Zorn
so tief in die Erde,
daß es bis an den Leib hineinfuhr;
35 dann packte es in seiner Wut
den linken Fuß
und riß sich selbst mitten ent-
　　zwei.

The third day
the messenger came back
and related:
"I haven't been able to find a single
*　　new name,*
but as I came to a high mountain
*　　around the forest 'corner,'*
where fox and hare say good night to
*　　each other,*
there I saw a little house,
and in front of the house burned a
*　　fire,*
and around the fire jumped
a little man who was just too ridicu-
*　　lous,*
hopped on one leg,
and screamed,
'Today I bake, tomorrow I brew,
day after tomorrow I'll fetch her
*　　child from the queen;*

oh, how good it is that nobody knows

that my name is Rumpelstiltskin.'"
*　　You can just imagine*
how happy the queen was
when she heard the name,
and when soon after that
the little man entered
and asked,

"Now, Madame Queen, what's my name?"

she asked first,
"Is your name Kunz?" — "No."
"Is your name Heinz?" — "No."
"Is it perhaps Rumpelstiltskin?"
"The Devil told you that,
the Devil told you that,"
screamed the little man
and rammed with his right foot,
because of anger,
so deep into the ground
that he went in up to the waist;
then in his rage he grabbed
his left foot
and tore himself in two, right up
*　　the middle.*

NOTES ON LANGUAGE

6 wo Fuchs und Hase sich gute Nacht
　sagen: *Saying used to express the*
　peacefulness of an isolated region.
32 vor Zorn: *The preposition* vor *is*
　often used to reveal emotion.
　Examples: Die Königin weinte vor
　Freude. Das Kind schrie vor Schmer-
　zen.

In referring to parts of the body,
a German prefers a definite article
to a possessive adjective:
31 mit dem rechten Fuß - *with his*
　right foot
34 an den Leib
36 den linken Fuß

WORDS AND WORD FAMILIES

der Bote -n (2)   der Teufel - (28, 29)
der Fuß/Füße (31, 36)   die Wut (35)
schreien [1a] (12, 30)   der Zorn (32)

COMMENTS ON GRAMMAR

Nominative, Accusative, Dative:

    The basic functions of these three cases are:
                  Nominative: subject
                  Accusative: direct object
                  Dative: indirect object
The cases are identified by characteristic forms and endings.

Case forms and endings of noun modifiers:

    The forms and endings of the modifying words differ for the three noun genders and for the plural.

    Case-and-number forms of the definite article:

	Masc.	Fem.	Neut.	Plur.
Nom.	der	die	das	die
Acc.	den	die	das	die
Dat.	dem	der	dem	den

    Case-and-number endings of the der-words: **dies-** - this, the latter; **jen-** - that, the former; **jed-** - each, every (as in **jeden Tag**); **all-** - all, every (as in **alle zehn Tage**); **manch-** - some, many a; **solch-** - such, such a; **welch-** - which, what a:

	Masc.	Fem.	Neut.	Plur.
Nom.	-er	-e	-es	-e
Acc.	-en	-e	-es	-e
Dat.	-em	-er	-em	-en

    Case endings of the indefinite article **ein** (singular only):

	Masc.	Fem.	Neut.
Nom.	—	-e	—
Acc.	-en	-e	—
Dat.	-em	-er	-em

    Case-and-number endings of the ein-words: **kein-** and the possessives: **mein-, dein-, sein-, ihr-** - her, **unser-/unsr-, euer-/eur-, ihr-** - their, **Ihr-** - your:

	Masc.	Fem.	Neut.	Plur.
Nom.	—	-e	—	-e
Acc.	-en	-e	—	-e
Dat.	-em	-er	-em	-e

    Case forms of the personal pronouns:

Nom.	ich	du	er	sie	es	wir	ihr	sie
Acc.	mich	dich	ihn	sie	es	uns	euch	sie
Dat.	mir	dir	ihm	ihr	ihm	uns	euch	ihnen

Name _____   Datum _____

Identify all underlined nouns and pronouns as to whether they
are nominative (subject), accusative (direct object), or dative
(indirect object). Put an "N" above each nominative, an "A"
above each accusative, a "D" above each dative noun or pronoun.

                 N   A
1 Der König wollte die Müllerstochter auf die Probe stellen.

2 Als sie zu ihm gebracht wurde, führte er sie in eine Kammer

   und gab ihr Rad und Haspel.

3 Er sagte zu ihr: „Wenn du bis morgen früh dieses Stroh nicht

   zu Gold versponnen hast, so mußt du sterben."

4 Darauf schloß er die Kammer zu, und sie blieb allein darin.

5 Da ging auf einmal die Tür auf, und ein kleines Männchen trat

   herein.

6 In zwei Nächten nahm das Männchen ein Halsband und einen Ring.

7 Am zweiten Abend sagte der König: „Dieses Stroh mußt du noch

   in dieser Nacht verspinnen."

8 Er dachte: „Eine reichere Frau finde ich in der ganzen Welt

   nicht.

9 Dem Männlein mußte die Müllerstochter ihr erstes Kind ver-

   sprechen.

10 Als am Morgen der König kam, fand er alles, wie er es ge-

   wünscht hatte.

11 Nach einem Jahr brachte die Königin ein schönes Kind zur Welt.

12 Die Königin bot dem Männchen alle Reichtümer des Königsreichs

   an, wenn es ihr das Kind lassen wollte.

13 Sie schickte einen Boten über Land.

14 Die ungewöhnlichsten und seltsamsten Namen sagte sie dem

   Männlein vor.

15 Der Bote erzählte: „Keinen einzigen neuen Namen habe ich fin-

   den können.

16 „Ich sah ein kleines Haus, und vor dem Haus brannte ein Feuer,
   und um das Feuer sprang ein lächerliches Männchen.

17 Da könnt ihr denken, wie die Königin froh war, als sie den
   Namen hörte.

18 Das hat dir der Teufel gesagt!

19 Es packte in seiner Wut den linken Fuß und riß sich selbst
   entzwei.

20 Der König, die Königin und ihr Kind lebten lang und glücklich in ihrem Schloß.

Review:

Rewrite the following sentences in the present tense:

1 Der Bote sah ein kleines Haus. [4b]

----

2 Vor dem Haus brannte ein Feuer. [§6.1.2]

----

3 Um das Feuer sprang ein lächerliches Männchen. [3a]

----

4 Es hüpfte auf einem Bein und schrie. [1a]

----

5 Es stieß mit dem rechten Fuß tief in die Erde. [7e]

----

6 Es riß sich selbst mitten entzwei. [1b]

PHYSIK UND CHEMIE

WAS IST NYLON?	WHAT IS NYLON?

Die erste Faser,
die ganz und gar synthetisch, also
    künstlich, hergestellt wurde,
war das Nylon.
Es wurde im Jahre 1938 in den USA
    auf den Markt gebracht.
5   Nylon war das Ergebnis von Ver-
    suchen,

mit denen erforscht werden sollte,

warum sich gewisse Moleküle zu
    „Riesenmolekülen" vereinigen,
wie im Gummi und in der Baumwolle.
10 Eines Tages
erhielt man ein Produkt,
das sich wie geschmolzener Zucker
    zu Fäden ausziehen ließ.
Nach dem Abkühlen
konnten die Fäden noch weiter ge-
    streckt werden;
15 dabei
wurden sie elastisch
und weniger leicht zerreißbar.
Das veranlaßte die Chemiker,
weitere Versuche damit anzustellen
20 und zu prüfen,
ob sich dieses neue Material nicht
    für die Herstellung neuer
    Textilfasern eignete.
Acht Jahre lang arbeiteten sie,
bis die neue Faser,
die den Namen Nylon bekam,
25 allen Ansprüchen genügte.

The first fiber
which was produced completely syn-
*   thetically, i.e. artificially,*
was nylon.
It was put on the market in the USA
*   in 1938.*
*   Nylon was the result of experi-*
*   ments*
with which it was supposed to be in-
*   vestigated*
why certain molecules combine into
*   "giant molecules,"*
as in rubber and in cotton.
One day
a product was obtained
which could be drawn out into threads
*   like melted sugar.*
After cooling off
the threads could be stretched still
*   further;*
thereby (as a result)
they became elastic
and less easily capable of being torn.
That caused the chemists
to set up further experiments with it
and to test
whether this new material wasn't suit-
*   able for the production of new*
*   textile fibers.*
They worked for eight years,
until the new fiber,
which received the name nylon,
satisfied all requirements.

NOTES ON LANGUAGE

Passive constructions are very com-
mon in German scientific style. The
passive verb phrase, a form of werden
+ past participle, occurs in the
following segments:
2 hergestellt wurde - *was produced*
6 erforscht werden sollte - *was sup-*
posed to be investigated
4 wurde...gebracht - *was brought*
14 konnten...gestreckt werden -
could be stretched.

The passive is so often needed
that several alternative construc-
tions have been developed. Two
alternatives of the passive occur
in this passage:
11 man erhielt ein Produkt - *a prod-*
uct was obtained (man + 3rd pers.
sing. verb + direct object which
is an inanimate thing)
12 das sich zu Fäden ausziehen ließ -
which could be drawn out to
threads (inanimate thing as sub-
ject + lassen + sich + infinitive)

WORDS AND WORD FAMILIES

der Faden/Fäden (12, 14)
die Faser -n (1, 23)
her·stellen (2)
   die Herstellung (21)

die Kunst/Künste
   künstlich (2)
der Versuch -e (5, 19)

COMMENTS ON GRAMMAR

Prepositions:

Prepositions are words used with nouns or pronouns to form prepositional phrases. In German, a noun or pronoun used with a given preposition is in a specific case.

Nouns and pronouns used with the following prepositions are in the accusative case: **bis, durch, für, gegen, ohne, um, wider.**

Dative forms are used with the prepositions: **aus, außer, bei, mit, nach, seit, von, zu.**

Conjunctions:

Conjunctions are words that make connections. There are two kinds of conjunctions: coordinating and subordinating.

Coordinating conjunctions:

Coordinating conjunctions, like und, aber, oder, denn, connect two main clauses. Examples:

> Die Tür ging auf, und der König trat herein.
> Es ist Mitte Januar, aber es liegt kein Schnee auf den Feldern.
> Du spinnst das Stroh zu Gold, oder du stirbst.
> Nylon ist eine synthetische Faser, denn es wird künstlich her-
>   gestellt.

Subordinating conjunctions:

Subordinating conjunctions connect a subordinate clause with a main clause. Typical subordinating conjunctions are:

> als - *when, referring to a single past event; as*
> bevor - *before*
> da - *since, in view of the fact that*
> damit - *so that, in order that*
> daß - *that*
> ehe - *before*
> indem - *while, as* [§8.4.1.2]
> nachdem - *after*
> ob - *whether (or not), if*
> während - *during the time that, while*
> weil - *because, due to the fact that*
> wenn - *if; when, whenever, referring to repeated events in the past*

Question words are also used as subordinating conjunctions, for example: **wann, warum, was, wer, wie, wo.**

Example sentences:

> Die Müllerstochter erschrak, als sie das Männchen sah.
> Da die neue Faser allen Ansprüchen genügte, wurde sie auf den
>   Markt gebracht.
> Man weiß, daß die Chemiker acht Jahre lang arbeiteten.
> Sie mußten prüfen, ob Nylon sich ausziehen ließ.
> Endlich fanden sie, was sie suchten.
> Dies ist das Laboratorium, wo man das neue Produkt erhalten hat.
> Es sollte erforscht werden, warum sich gewisse Moleküle zu
>   „Riesenmolekülen" vereinigen.

Reminder: the inflected verb stands at the end of a subordinate clause, and all subordinate clauses are set off by commas.

Name _____ Datum _____

Connect each pair of sentences with the coordinating or subordinating conjunction in parentheses. If the conjunction is
given first, it is to be used with the first clause; if last,
with the second. *(First of two exercises.)*

1 (bevor) Nylon wurde auf den Markt gebracht. Es mußte geprüft

   werden. <u>Bevor Nylon auf den Markt gebracht wurde, mußte es geprüft werden.</u>

2 Nylon ist ein amerikanisches Produkt. Es wurde zuerst in den

   USA hergestellt. (denn)

   ----

3 (nachdem) Die Chemiker hatten acht Jahre lang an diesem Pro-

   dukt gearbeitet. Sie brachten es auf den Markt.

   ----

4 Nylon wurde künstlich hergestellt. Es konnte in den USA auf

   den Markt gebracht werden. (damit)

   ----

5 Gewisse Moleküle vereinigen sich zu „Riesenmolekülen". Die

   Chemiker wollten wissen, warum. (und)

   ----

6 Die Chemiker mußten lange Zeit forschen. Sie erhielten ein

   gutes Produkt. (bevor)

   ----

7 (nachdem) Dieses Produkt war abgekühlt worden. Die Fäden

   konnten noch weiter gestreckt werden. (war...worden - *had been*)

   ----

8 Die Chemiker sahen. Die Fäden wurden elastisch und weniger
  zerreißbar. (daß)

------------------------- --.--

----

9 (als) Sie erkannten das. Sie stellten weitere Versuche an.

----

10 Sie wollten prüfen: „Eignet sich dieses neue Material für die
   Herstellung neuer Textilfasern?" (ob)

Review the case forms on page 22 and write phrases with the following prepositions and nouns or pronouns. Translate each phrase.

  1 ohne (er) ____ohne ihn_____   _____*without him*_____

  2 mit (ich) _____   _____

  3 außer (die Königin) _____

     ----

  4 bis (nächste Woche) _____

     ----

  5 seit (ein Monat) _____

     ----

  6 für (sein Versuch) _____

     ----

  7 von (ihr) _____   _____

  8 zu (Sie) _____   _____

  9 bei (wir) _____   _____

 10 gegen (sie) _____   _____

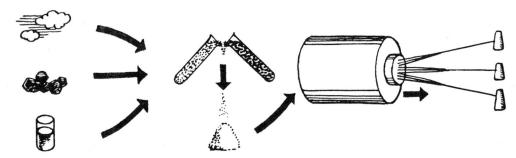

Das Nylon wird aus vier häufig
    vorkommenden Elementen her-
    gestellt:
  aus Kohlenstoff,
  Wasserstoff,
  Stickstoff
5 und Sauerstoff.
  Der Kohlenstoff ist in der Kohle
    enthalten,
  Stickstoff und Sauerstoff
  in der Luft
  und Wasserstoff im Wasser.
10 Bei der Herstellung des Nylons
  werden Kohle, Erdöl, Erdgas, Kalk,
    Wasser, Steinsalz und Luft
    gebraucht.
  In Amerika verwendet man dazu auch
    Haferspelze und Maiskolben.
  Nylon entsteht dadurch,
  daß zwei verschiedene Molekülarten
15 zu großen Molekülen vereinigt wer-
    den.
  Die anfangs noch kleinen Molekül-
    verbindungen
  ergeben zunächst
  eine Zwischenstufe,
  das „Nylonsalz".
20 Wenn dies Nylonsalz in großen Druck-
    kesseln erhitzt wird,
  haken sich die Moleküle zusammen
  und bilden lange Ketten,
  das „Polymer".
  Es ist eine in der Hitze zähe
    Flüssigkeit,
25 die unter hohem Druck durch Spinn-
    düsen (winzig kleine Löcher in
    einer Metallplatte) hindurch-
    gepreßt wird.
  Die heraustretenden Fasern erhärten
  beim Abkühlen
  und werden zu einem Faden zusammen-
    gefaßt.
  Nachdem dieser Faden
30 auf drei- bis vierfache Länge ge-
    streckt worden ist,
  wird er zerreißfest und elastisch,
  und wir haben den fertigen Nylon-
    faden.

*Nylon is produced from four ele-
    ments which occur frequently
    (in nature):*
from carbon,
hydrogen,
nitrogen,
and oxygen.

Carbon is contained in coal,

nitrogen and oxygen
in the air,
and hydrogen in water.
In the production of nylon

coal, petroleum, natural gas, lime,
    water, and rock salt are used.

In America oat chaff and corn cobs
    are also used.
  Nylon results from the fact
that two different kinds of molecules

are combined into macro-molecules.

*The molecular compounds, which ini-
    tially are still small,*
yield first of all
an intermediate stage,
"nylon salt."
When this nylon salt is heated in big
    pressure boilers,
the molecules hook together
and form long chains,
the "polymer."
It is a fluid which is viscous when
    hot,

which is forced under high pressure
    through spinning nozzles (tiny
    little holes in a metal plate).

The emerging fibers harden
in the process of cooling

and are combined into a thread.

After this thread
has been stretched to three or four
    times its length,
it becomes strong and elastic,
and we have the finished nylon
    thread.

NOTES ON LANGUAGE

The "extended adjective construction" is characteristic of German scientific style:

1 aus <u>vier</u> häufig vorkommenden <u>Elementen</u> - *out of <u>four</u> <u>elements</u> which occur frequently*

16 <u>die</u> anfangs noch kleinen <u>Molekülverbindungen</u> - *the molecular compounds, which at the beginning are still small,*

24 <u>eine</u> in der Hitze zähe <u>Flüssigkeit</u> - *a fluid which is viscous when hot*

WORDS AND WORD FAMILIES

ergeben [4a] (17)
   das Ergebnis/-nisse
die Kohle -n (6, 11)
   der Kohlenstoff (2, 6)

der Sauerstoff (5, 7)
der Stickstoff (4, 7)
verwenden (12)
der Wasserstoff (3, 9)

COMMENTS ON GRAMMAR

Relative clauses:

A relative clause is a subordinate clause that identifies or describes something — a person, a thing, a condition, an event — mentioned previously in the same sentence.

A relative clause is headed by a relative pronoun. The forms of the relative pronoun are:

	Masc.	Fem.	Neut.	Plur.
Nom.	der	die	das	die
Acc.	den	die	das	die
Dat.	dem	der	dem	denen

Notice that the forms are the same as for the definite article, except for the dative plural.

The formula for a relative clause is:

relative pronoun + subject + ... + inflected verb.

In the following examples of sentences with relative clauses, the relative pronoun is underscored with a broken line, the inflected verb of the relative clause with a solid line.

1 Das Nylon war die erste Faser, die man synthetisch herstellte.
2 Die Chemiker, die acht Jahre lang arbeiteten, gebrauchten vier Elemente.
3 Das Produkt, dem man den Namen Nylon gab, genügte allen Ansprüchen.
4 Das Nylonsalz, das eine Zwischenstufe ist, wird in Druckkesseln erhitzt.
5 Die vier Elemente, aus denen Nylon hergestellt wird, sind Kohlenstoff, Wasserstoff, Stickstoff und Sauerstoff.
6 Der Faden, der aus vielen Fasern zusammengefaßt worden ist, ist zerreißfest und elastisch.

The noun to which the relative pronoun refers is called the antecedent. In the example sentences the antecedents are:

1 Faser; 2 Chemiker; 3 Produkt; 4 Nylonsalz; 5 Elemente; 6 Faden.

A sentence with a relative clause can be expressed in two independent sentences. The two sentences in the first example are:

Das Nylon war die erste Faser. Man stellte sie (diese Faser) synthetisch her.

Conversely, two sentences, the second of which has a personal pronoun referring to an antecedent in the first, can be made into a single sentence with a relative clause. This can be done in three steps:

1 Replace the pronoun in the second sentence with the corresponding relative pronoun, using the following table:

	Masc.	Fem.	Neut.	Plur.
Nom.	er - der	sie - die	es - das	sie - die
Acc.	ihn - den	sie - die	es - das	sie - die
Dat.	ihm - dem	ihr - der	ihm - dem	ihnen - denen

2 Put the relative pronoun at the head of the clause and the inflected verb at the end. If the personal pronoun was in a prepositional phrase, the preposition remains with the relative pronoun:

aus ihnen - aus denen

3 Insert the relative clause immediately after the noun it refers to, unless the only word following that noun in the main clause is an infinitive or a past participle. These verb forms may intervene between the antecedent and the relative pronoun.

Reminder: all subordinate clauses are set off by commas.

Summary:

<table>
<tr><td>Two independent
sentences</td><td>Sentence with a
relative clause</td></tr>
<tr><td>Die Chemiker gebrauchten vier Elemente. Sie mußten acht Jahre lang arbeiten.</td><td>Die Chemiker, die acht Jahre lang arbeiten mußten, gebrauchten vier Elemente.</td></tr>
<tr><td>Das Nylonsalz wird in Druckkesseln erhitzt. Sie genügen allen technischen Ansprüchen.</td><td>Das Nylonsalz wird in Druckkesseln erhitzt, die allen technischen Ansprüchen genügen.</td></tr>
</table>

Name _____ Datum _____

Rewrite each pair of sentences as one, making a relative clause out of the second.

1 Nylon wird künstlich hergestellt. Es wurde im Jahre 1938 auf den Markt gebracht. _____ Das Nylon, das 1938 auf den Markt ___ _____ gebracht wurde, wird künstlich hergestellt. _____

2 Das Nylon wird aus vier Elementen hergestellt. Sie kommen häufig in der Natur vor.

----

3 Die Molekülverbindungen ergeben zunächst eine Zwischenstufe. Sie sind anfangs noch klein.

----

4 Die Moleküle bilden das „Polymer". Sie haken sich in langen Ketten zusammen.

----

5 Das „Polymer" ist eine Flüssigkeit. Sie ist in der Hitze zäh.

----

6 Die heraustretenden Fasern werden zu einem Faden zusammengefaßt. Sie erhärten beim Abkühlen.

In the following sentences, underline the relative pronoun twice, the inflected verb in the relative clause once.

1 Das Material, das man aus vier Elementen hergestellt hatte, eignete sich für neue Textilien.

2 Eines Tages erhielt man ein Produkt, das sich zu Fäden ausziehen ließ.

3 Die neue Faser, die den Namen Nylon bekam, genügte allen Ansprüchen.

4 Polymer ist eine Flüssigkeit, die unter hohem Druck durch
  Spinndüsen hindurchgepreßt wird.

5 Das ist eine Kunst, die mir wohl gefällt.

6 Das Männchen nahm den Ring, den das Mädchen ihm gegeben hatte.

In the following sentences, rewrite the relative clause as an
independent sentence, using the corresponding personal pronoun
instead of the relative pronoun.

1 Das Material, das man aus vier Elementen hergestellt hatte,
  eignete sich für neue Textilien.
  _____Man hatte es aus vier Elementen hergestellt._____

2 Eines Tages erhielt man ein Produkt, das sich zu Fäden ausziehen ließ.

  _____

3 Die neue Faser, die den Namen Nylon bekam, genügte allen Ansprüchen.

  _____

4 Polymer ist eine Flüssigkeit, die unter hohem Druck durch
  Spinndüsen hindurchgepreßt wird.

  _____

  _____

Review:

Identify all underlined nouns and pronouns as to whether they
are nominative, accusative, or dative. Put an "N" above each
nominative, an "A" above each accusative, a "D" above each
dative noun or pronoun.

1 Bei der Herstellung des Nylons werden Kohle, Erdöl, ... gebraucht.

2 In Amerika verwendet man dazu auch Haferspelze und Maiskolben.

3 Nylon entsteht dadurch, daß zwei verschiedene Molekülarten
  zu großen Molekülen vereinigt werden.

4 Die anfangs noch kleinen Molekülverbindungen ergeben zunächst
  eine Zwischenstufe, das „Nylonsalz".

Wie so viele andere Stoffe,
die der Mensch produziert
oder die Natur geschaffen hat,
kann auch Chlor schädlich oder
    nützlich sein.
5 Im ersten Weltkrieg
wurden schreckliche Giftgase aus
    Chlor verwendet.
Andererseits ist das Chlor
eines der besten Hilfsmittel zum
    Schutz der Gesundheit.
Chlor ist in vielen Desinfektions-
    mitteln enthalten.
10 In den meisten Trinkwasseranlagen
    der Städte
wird Chlor benutzt,
um Bakterien abzutöten,
die nach dem Filtern noch im Wasser
    enthalten sind.
Dafür genügen vier bis fünf Teile
    flüssiges Chlor auf eine
    Milliarde Teile Wasser.
15 Diese geringe Chlormenge im Trink-
    wasser
ist für uns nicht gesundheits-
    schädlich,
auch wenn das Wasser zuweilen nach
    Chlor riecht.
Chlor verbindet sich leicht
mit anderen Elementen;
20 darum
kommt es in der Natur nicht frei
    vor,
sondern nur in Verbindungen.
Die bekannteste Chlorverbindung
ist das Kochsalz,
25 das aus Chlor und Natrium besteht.

Da das Meerwasser zu etwa 3,5% aus
    Salz besteht,
sind in den Ozeanen riesige Mengen
    Chlor enthalten.

Like so many other materials
which man has produced
or nature has created,
chlorine, too, can be injurious or
    useful.
In the First World War
terrible poisonous gases made of
    chlorine were used.
On the other hand chlorine is
one of the best aids for the protec-
    tion of health.
Chlorine is contained in many disin-
    fectants.

In most city water systems

chlorine is used
to kill off bacteria
which are still contained in the wa-
    ter after filtering.
For that four to five parts of fluid
    chlorine to a billion parts of
    water is sufficient.
This small amount of chlorine in the
    drinking water

is not damaging to our health,

even if the water sometimes smells
    of chlorine.
Chlorine combines easily
with other elements;
therefore
it does not occur uncombined in na-
    ture,
but only in compounds.
The best-known chlorine compound
is table salt,
which consists of chlorine and so-
    dium.
Since sea-water consists of about
    3.5% salt,
huge amounts of chlorine are con-
    tained in the oceans.

NOTES ON LANGUAGE

Look at the following example:
21 kommt es in der Natur nicht frei
vor,...
In order to understand this seg-
ment, you must know that the com-
plete verb is vorkommen. *If you*
stop at kommen *and look it up in*
the dictionary, you will not find
a meaning that will help you to

understand this context.
A careful distinction must be
made between prepositions in prep-
ositional phrases and the separa-
ble components of compound verbs
which look like prepositions:
an, auf, mit, nach, vor, zu, *for*
example. A <u>preposition</u> *is fol-*
lowed by a noun or pronoun,

whereas the <u>*separable parts of*</u>
<u>*verbs*</u> *are at the end of the clause,*
followed only occasionally by
an afterthought.
   Study the following usages:

Prepositional phrases:

Er sagte <u>zu ihm</u>:
Jetzt mache dich <u>an die Arbeit</u>.

Er setzt sich <u>vor das Rädchen</u>.

Die Königin besann sich <u>auf alle</u>
<u>Namen</u>.

Compound verbs:

Darauf <u>schloß</u> er die Kammer <u>zu</u>.
Das Männchen <u>fing</u> wieder <u>an</u> zu
   schnurren.
Sie <u>sagte</u> dem Männchen die selt-
   samsten Namen <u>vor</u>.
Da <u>ging</u> auf einmal die Tür <u>auf</u>.

WORDS AND WORD FAMILIES

bestehen [§6.2.2] (aus) (25, 26)
enthalten [7a] (9, 13, 27)
die Gesundheit (8)
   gesundheitsschädlich (16)
die Menge -n (27)
   die Chlormenge (15)
das Mittel -:
   das Hilfsmittel (8)
   das Desinfektionsmittel (9)

nicht...sondern (21-22)
nützlich (4)
   benutzen (11)
schädlich (4)
   gesundheitsschädlich (16)
verbinden (18)
   die Verbindung -en (22)
   die Chlorverbindung (23)
vor·kommen [5d] (21)

COMMENTS ON GRAMMAR

The passive verb phrase:

    The passive verb phrase is used in all styles of German, but it is especially common in scientific writings. It consists of an inflected form of the auxiliary **werden** + the past participle of the main verb.

    The inflected present and past tense forms of **werden** are used as the passive auxiliary in the present and past passive verb phrases:

Present		Past	
werde	werden	wurde	wurden
wirst	werdet	wurdest	wurdet
wird	werden	wurde	wurden

Examples:

Chlor <u>wird</u> in Trinkwasseranlagen der Städte <u>benutzt</u>. *(is used)*
Chlor <u>wird</u> von der Natur <u>geschaffen</u> und <u>wurde</u> dann von Menschen
    <u>produziert</u>. *(is created...was produced)*
Weitere Versuche <u>wurden</u> von den Chemikern <u>angestellt</u>. *(were carried out)*
Im ersten Weltkrieg <u>wurden</u> Giftgase aus Chlor <u>verwendet</u>. *(were used)*

    The perfect passive verb phrase consists of an inflected form of **sein** + ... + past participle of the main verb + the special passive participle **worden**.
    Examples:

Die Bakterien <u>sind</u> schon <u>abgetötet worden</u>. *(have been killed)*
Im ersten Weltkrieg <u>ist</u> ein Giftgas aus Chlor <u>verwendet worden</u>. *(was used)*
Du <u>bist</u> vom König zu seiner Gemahlin <u>gemacht worden</u>. *(have been made)*
Durch größere Chlormengen <u>sind</u> wir <u>beschädigt worden</u>. *(We have been
    harmed by rather large amounts of chlorine.)*

    The future passive verb phrase consists of an inflected form of **werden** (as the future auxiliary) + ... + past participle of the main verb + the infinitive **werden** (as the passive auxiliary).
    Examples:

Die Gesundheit <u>wird</u> durch diese Desinfektionsmittel vor Bakterien <u>ge-
    schützt werden</u>. (wird + werden: *future;* geschützt werden: *passive -
    will be protected*)
Bei der Herstellung des Nylons <u>werden</u> Kohle, Erdöl, Erdgas und Kalk
    <u>gebraucht werden</u>. *(will be used)*

    The past participle of the main verb + infinitive **werden** is also used in combination with the modal auxiliaries.
    Examples:

Es <u>sollte</u> <u>erforscht werden</u>. *(was to be investigated)*
Die Fäden <u>können</u> weiter <u>gestreckt werden</u>. *(can be stretched)*
Zwei Molekülarten <u>mußten</u> <u>vereinigt werden</u>. *(had to be combined)*

    The passive describes a process.
    If the process is carried out by human beings, **von** + dative is used:

Nylon wurde um das Jahr 1930 <u>von den Chemikern</u> hergestellt. *(by the
    chemists)*

If the process involves a means or device, **durch** + accusative is used:

Durch ganz kleine Chlormengen kann Trinkwasser unschädlich gemacht werden.
   (by means of quite small quantities of chlorine)
Chlorgas kann durch Abkühlung oder durch Druck in Flüssigkeit verwandelt
   werden. *(Chlorine gas can be changed into fluid by cooling or by
   pressure.)*
Der Brief wurde durch Boten geschickt. *(The letter was sent by messenger.)*

The meaning of a passive verb phrase can often be expressed by an "active" sentence. Compare:

Active	Passive
1 Um das Jahr 1930 haben die Che-miker Nylon hergestellt.	Nylon ist um das Jahr 1930 von den Chemikern hergestellt worden.
2 Ganz kleine Chlormengen können Trinkwasser unschädlich machen.	Durch ganz kleine Chlormengen kann Trinkwasser unschädlich gemacht werden.
3 Man hat diesen Faden auf drei- bis vierfache Länge gestreckt.	Dieser Faden ist auf drei- bis vier-fache Länge gestreckt worden.

Summary:

Active	Passive
Subject (Nom.)	**von** + dat. *(see Ex. 1)* **durch** + acc. *(Ex. 2)*
Man	*(Ex. 3)*
Inflected verb	**werden** + participle
Direct object (Acc.)	Subject (Nom.)

Name _____ Datum _____

Rewrite the following active sentences as passives.

1 Man brachte Nylon im Jahre 1938 auf den Markt.

____Nylon wurde im Jahre 1938 auf den Markt gebracht._____

   (Notice that man *does not appear in the passive sentence.)*

2 Nach dem Abkühlen konnte man die Fäden noch weiter strecken.

_____

_____

3 Die Chemiker haben weitere Versuche angestellt.

_____

_____

4 In Amerika verwendet man dazu auch Haferspelze und Maiskolben.

_____

_____

5 Man hat die heraustretenden Fasern zu einem Faden zusammengefaßt.

_____

_____

6 Man preßte die Flüssigkeit durch Spinndüsen hindurch.

_____

_____

Rewrite the following passive sentences as active constructions.

1 Dieser Faden wird auf drei- bis vierfache Länge gestreckt.

____Man streckt diesen Faden auf drei- bis vierfache Länge._____

   (Notice that since no specific agent or means was mentioned in the passive,
man *must be supplied in the active sentence.)*

2 Das Nylonsalz ist in großen Druckkesseln erhitzt worden.

_____

_____

3 Dieser Stoff wird vom Menschen nicht produziert werden.

_____

_____

4 Im ersten Weltkrieg wurden Giftgase aus Chlor verwendet.

----

5 Dieses Produkt konnte zu Fäden ausgezogen werden.

----

6 In Trinkwasseranlagen soll Chlor benutzt werden, um Bakterien
  abzutöten.

Review:

In the following sentences, underline the subject(s) of the main
clause once, the subject(s) of any subordinate clause(s) twice.

1 Wie so viele andere Stoffe, die der Mensch produziert oder

  die Natur geschaffen hat, kann auch Chlor schädlich oder nütz-

  lich sein.

2 In den meisten Trinkwasseranlagen der Städte wird Chlor be-

  nutzt, um Bakterien abzutöten, die nach dem Filtern noch im

  Wasser enthalten sind.

3 Dafür genügen vier bis fünf Teile flüssiges Chlor auf eine

  Milliarde Teile Wasser.

4 Diese geringe Chlormenge im Trinkwasser ist für uns nicht ge-

  sundheitsschädlich, auch wenn das Wasser zuweilen nach Chlor

  riecht.

5 Da das Meerwasser zu etwa 3,5% aus Salz besteht, sind in den

  Ozeanen riesige Mengen Chlor enthalten.

Reines Chlor ist
ein erstickend riechendes grünlich-
    gelbes Gas.
Es wurde zuerst von dem Chemiker
    Scheel im Jahre 1774 darge-
    stellt.
Im Jahre 1810 stellte Humphry Davy
    fest,
5 daß es ein Element ist.
Heute wird es billig und in großen
    Mengen aus Kochsalzlösung
    gewonnen,
durch die ein elektrischer Strom
    hindurchgeschickt wird.
Man nennt dies Verfahren Elektro-
    lyse.
Chlorgas kann durch Abkühlung oder
    durch Druck in Flüssigkeit
    verwandelt werden.
10 In dieser Form wird es in eisernen
    Behältern oder in Spezialtank-
    wagen verschickt.
Chlor wird zum Bleichen benutzt;
besonders
bei der Papierfabrikation
wird es in großen Mengen gebraucht.
15 Chlor ist ein wichtiger Bestand-
    teil
moderner antiseptischer und Betäu-
    bungsmittel,
zum Beispiel des Chloroforms.
In vielen Sekreten des menschlichen
    Körpers
sind Chlorsalze enthalten.
20 Zum Beispiel enthält der Magensaft
    Salzsäure,
eine Verbindung von Chlor und Was-
    serstoff.
Auch im Schweiß
sind Chlorsalze enthalten;
darum schmeckt er salzig.

Pure chlorine is
a greenish-yellow gas that has a suf-
    focating odor.

It was first described by the chemist
    Scheel in 1774.

In the year 1810 Humphry Davy estab-
    lished the fact
that it is an element.
Today it is obtained cheaply and in
    large amounts from salt solu-
    tion
through which an electric current is
    sent.

This process is called electrolysis.

Chlorine gas can be changed into
    fluid by cooling or by pressure.

In this form it is transported in
    iron containers or in special
    tank cars.
Chlorine is used for bleaching;
especially
in the manufacture of paper
it is used in large quantities.

Chlorine is an important component

of modern antiseptics and anesthetics,

for example, of chloroform.

In many secretions of the human body

chlorine salts are contained.
For example, the gastric juice con-
    tains hydrochloric acid,

a compound of chlorine and hydrogen.

In perspiration, too,
chlorine salts are contained;
for that reason it tastes salty.

NOTES ON LANGUAGE

8 dies = dieses

The infinitive as noun:
The infinitive form can be used as
a noun. All these nouns are neuter,
and like other nouns they are capi-
talized. Examples:

8 dieses Verfahren
11 zum Bleichen
   nach dem Abkühlen
   beim Abkühlen

Note the idiomatic usages of
prepositions with infinitive
nouns:

zum - *for (the purpose of)*
beim - *in (the act or process of)*

The infinitive is usually trans-
lated into English with an -ing
form of the verb: zum Bleichen -
for (the purpose of) bleaching.

WORDS AND WORD FAMILIES

behalten [7a]
    der Behälter - (10)
das Beispiel -e (17, 20)
der Druck (8)
    der Druckkessel -

gebrauchen (14)
riechen (nach) (2)
schicken:
    hindurch·schicken (7)
    verschicken (10)

COMMENTS ON GRAMMAR

The genitive case:

Forms:

	Masc.	Fem.	Neut.	Plur.
The definite article:	des	der	des	der
The indefinite article:	eines	einer	eines	
Endings of kein-, *the possessives, and the* der-*words:*	-es	-er	-es	-er

Genitive endings of nouns:

Masculine and neuter singular nouns: -es/-s
Weak masculine nouns: -en/-n [See §2.3, §2.4]
Feminine singular and all plural nouns: <u>no</u> *genitive endings.*

Examples:

In Trinkwasseranlagen <u>der</u> Städte wird Chlor benutzt.
In vielen Sekreten <u>des</u> menschlichen <u>Körpers</u> sind Chlorsalze enthalten.
Das Chlor ist eines <u>der</u> besten <u>Hilfsmittel</u> zum Schutz <u>der</u> Gesundheit.
Chlor ist ein wichtiger Bestandteil moder<u>ner</u> antiseptisch<u>er</u> (Mittel)
    und Betäubungsmittel, zum Beispiel <u>des</u> Chlorof<u>orms</u>.

For uses of the genitive, see §1.4.

Plural forms of nouns:

For a listing of noun plural forms, see §3.1-4.

There are a few rules of thumb that may help you to learn the plurals of nouns.

1 With few exceptions, feminine noun plurals have **-n/-en**.

2 Masculine and neuter nouns ending in **-el/-en/-er** have no ending in the plural. Sometimes the main vowel has umlaut.

3 Otherwise the most common ending for both masculine and neuter nouns is **-e**. Often the masculine nouns in this group have umlaut.

Dative plural forms:

Except for the nouns with the plural ending **-s**, all dative plural nouns end in **-n**.

Examples:

Nom.	die Tage	Nom.	die Hände
Dat.	in den Tagen	Dat.	in den Händen
Nom.	die Verbindungen	Nom.	die Mäntel
Dat.	bei den Verbindungen	Dat.	mit den Mänteln
Nom.	die Götter	Nom.	die Hotels
Dat.	von den Göttern	Dat.	in den Hotels

Name _____   Datum _____

Make a nominative + genitive noun phrase out of each pair of
nouns given. Translate each phrase into English.

1 die Fäden / der Zucker _die Fäden des Zuckers - *the threads of sugar*_

2 die Probleme / die Herstellung _____

_____

3 die Versuche / die Chemiker _____

_____

4 das Abkühlen / das Produkt _____

_____

5 die Riesenmoleküle / die Baumwolle _____

_____

6 die Fasern / der Stoff _____

_____

7 die Moleküle / der Sauerstoff _____

_____

8 die langen Ketten / die Moleküle _____

_____

Give the nominative plural of each of the following noun phrases.
Then form a prepositional phrase with the plural noun, using the
preposition in parentheses, and translate your phrase into English. The plural ending is supplied for each noun.

1 das Jahr -e (in + dative) _die Jahre - in den Jahren - *in the years*_

2 dieses Produkt -e (ohne) _____

_____

3 keine Verbindung -en (zu) _____

_____

4 eine Zwischenstufe -n (durch) _____

_____

5 unser Druckkessel - (mit) _____

_____

6 das Loch/Löcher (in + accusative) _____

_____

7 der Ozean -e (auf + dative) _____

_____

8 dieser Bestandteil -e (mit) _____

_____

Review:

Rewrite the following passive sentences as active sentences.
Reminder: When no agent is mentioned in the passive, **man** must
be supplied as the subject of the active sentence.

1 Chlor wurde von dem Chemiker Scheel dargestellt.

_____

2 Heute wird es billig aus Kochsalzlösung gewonnen.

_____

3 Durch die Kochsalzlösung wird ein elektrischer Strom hindurch-
  geschickt.

_____

_____

4 Chlor wird zum Bleichen benutzt.

_____

MENSCH UND GESELLSCHAFT

ICH BIN SCHWEIZER

Ich bin Schweizer.
Wenn ich meiner Mutter sage:
„Ich gehe nach Deutschland"
oder „Ich gehe nach Frankreich"
5 oder „Ich gehe nach Schweden",
dann sagt sie:
„Du gehst also ins Ausland."
   Für die Schweizer gibt es zwei
     Welten:
das Inland und das Ausland.
10 Wenn ich ins Ausland gehe,
sagt meine Mutter:
„Paß auf,
daß dir nichts gestohlen wird,
gib deinen Koffer nicht aus der
     Hand."
15 Schweizer tragen im Ausland ihr
     Geld
in Beuteln unter dem Hemd
oder eingenäht in die Unterwäsche.
   Für uns hat das Wort Ausland
     immer noch

den Klang von Elend.

20   Wenn ich dort sage:
„Ich bin Schweizer",
erwarte ich etwas,
einen Ausruf des Erstaunens,
Überraschung,
25 Hochachtung
oder wenigstens Freundlichkeit.
   Während meines Berlinaufent-
     haltes
passierte ich oft den Grenzüber-
     gang
zwischen West- und Ostberlin.
30 Man hat dort das Gefühl,

in eine andere Welt zu kommen,

man empfindet Angst,
man geht ins Unbekannte.
   Mir fiel auf,
35 daß ich an diesem Übergang immer
     viele Schweizer sah.
Ich sprach nicht mit ihnen,
und sie sprachen nicht,
und ich wußte doch,
daß es Schweizer sind.
40   Andere Nationalitäten

nehmen ihren Paß erst vor dem Be-
     amten aus der Tasche

oder tragen ihn unauffällig in
     der Hand;
die Schweizer aber tragen ihren
     Paß gut sichtbar,

I AM A SWISS

I am a Swiss.
When I tell my mother,
"I'm going to Germany,"
or "I'm going to France,"
or "I'm going to Sweden,"
she says,
"So, you're going abroad."
   For the Swiss people there are
     two worlds:
home and abroad.
When I go abroad
my mother says,
"Watch out
that nothing is stolen from you;

don't part with your suitcase."

Abroad, the Swiss carry their money

in pouches under their shirts
or sewn into their underwear.
   For us the word "abroad" still
     has
the sound of "exile" (and therefore
     "misery," its modern meaning).
   When I say there (abroad),
"I am a Swiss,"
I expect something:
an exclamation of astonishment,
surprise,
respect,
or at least friendliness.

   During my stay in Berlin

I often crossed the border

between West and East Berlin.
One has the feeling there
that one is getting into another
     world;
one feels anxiety,
one is going into the unknown.
   It struck me
that I always saw a lot of Swiss at
     this border.
I didn't speak with them,
and they didn't speak,
and I nevertheless knew
that they were Swiss.
   Other nationalities
don't take their passports out of
     their pockets until they are in
     front of the official,
or they carry it inconspicuously in
     their hand;
the Swiss, however, carry their pass-
     ports (where they are) visible,

45 ihren roten Paß	their red passport
mit dem weißen Kreuz.	with the white cross.
Er soll sie schützen,	It is supposed to protect them,
und die Tatsache, daß sie Schweizer sind,	and the fact that they are Swiss
soll die Gefahr abwenden,	is supposed to avert danger,
50 soll ihnen Vorteile bringen	is supposed to bring them advantages
sogar hier bei ostdeutschen Volks- polizisten,	even here, with the East German State Police,
die sie nicht zu ihren Freunden zählen.	whom they don't count among their friends.
Ich bin Schweizer.	I am a Swiss.
Das hat also mehr zu bedeuten	That has, then, more significance
55 als einfach die Antwort auf die Frage:	than simply the answer to the ques- tion,
„Woher kommen Sie?"	"Where do you come from?"

NOTES ON LANGUAGE

*Common contractions of preposition
+ definite article:*
10 ins (= in das) Ausland
15 im (= in dem) Ausland
33 ins Unbekannte
*Some others of the common contrac-
tions are:*
am = an dem
ans = an das
vom = von dem
zum = zu dem
zur = zu der
*Notice the differences in form and
meaning:*
Wir gehen ins Ausland.
Wir wohnen im Ausland.

*Reminder: When referring to parts
of the body and to clothing, the
German prefers the definite article to the possessive:*
14 aus der Hand
42 in der Hand
16 unter dem Hemd
17 in die Unterwäsche
41 aus der Tasche

*Reminder: Pronouns must agree
with their antecedents in gender
and number. The pronouns ihn in
segment 42 and Er, 47, both refer
to the noun Paß, segments 41 and
45.*

WORDS AND WORD FAMILIES

die Angst (32)
auf·fallen [7a] (34)
   unauffällig (42)
auf·passen (12)
das Ausland (7, 9, 10, 18)

der Paß/Pässe (41, 43, 45)
tragen [6a] (15, 42, 43)
der Übergang/-gänge (35)
   der Grenzübergang (28)
die Welt -en (8, 31)

COMMENTS ON GRAMMAR

Prefixed verbs:

There is a small group of prefixes which are attached to root verbs: **be-, emp-, ent-, er-, ge-, miß-, ver-, zer-**; the prepositions **durch, über, um, unter, wider** are sometimes found as prefixes to root verbs.
Examples:

deuten / bedeuten	brechen / zerbrechen
finden / empfinden	
stehen / entstehen	schauen / durchschauen
blicken / erblicken	setzen / übersetzen
brauchen / gebrauchen	geben / umgeben
verstehen / mißverstehen	scheiden / unterscheiden
einigen / vereinigen	stehen / widerstehen

Three things must be noticed about these verbs with prefixes:

Form: The prefix is an integral part of the verb. These verbs have no past participle prefix **ge-**. Compare the following root verbs with their derivative prefixed verbs:

Root verbs		Prefixed verbs	
Infinitive	Past participle	Infinitive	Past participle
finden	gefunden	empfinden	empfunden
geben	gegeben	umgeben	umgeben
schauen	geschaut	durchschauen	durchschaut
scheiden	geschieden	unterscheiden	unterschieden

Pronunciation: The root part of the verb is accented in speaking: vereinigen, entstehen, übersetzen, widerlegen. (Exception: the verb mißverstehen, mißverstanden.)

Meaning: These prefixed verbs nearly always mean something different from the root verbs.

Compound verbs:

A very common construction consists of a root verb used in combination with a preposition (like **an, bei, mit**) or an adverb (like **ab, fort, weg, zusammen**). These words are an essential part of the total verb construction as to both meaning and grammatical form. Examples:

fallen / auf•fallen	kommen / her•kommen
fassen / zusammen•fassen	fangen / an•fangen

The separable component comes at the end of its clause. There are four combinations of the verb and the separable component.

1) The verb is inflected, and in an independent clause.

Chlor kommt in der Natur nicht frei vor.
Da ging die Tür auf.

2) The verb is inflected and stands at the end of a subordinate clause.

>   als das Männchen hereintrat,
>   bis sie endlich zu weinen anfing.

3) The verb is in the past participle form.

>   Die Fasern werden zusammengefaßt.
>   Die erste Faser, die künstlich hergestellt wurde,...

4) The verb is in the infinitive form. It may be with **zu**:

>   Das veranlaßte die Chemiker, weitere Versuche damit anzustellen und
>   zu prüfen,...

or without **zu**:

>   Der Paß soll die Gefahr abwenden.
>   Das Produkt ließ sich zu Fäden ausziehen.

Three things must be noticed about these compound verbs:

Form: The past participle prefix **ge-** and the infinitive
marker **zu** have a position between the separable component and
the root verb. See examples under 3) and 4) above.

Pronunciation: The separable part of the verb is accented
in speaking: anfangen, abwenden, zusammengefaßt, hereintrat,
anzustellen.

Meaning: Although the meaning of a compound verb is often
closer to its root verb than is the case with a prefixed verb,
care must be taken to look up the whole verb in the dictionary,
because many of these have unexpected meanings.

Note: The prepositions **durch, über, um, unter, wider** are
found in both lists: there are examples of their use in prefixed verbs and other examples of their use as separable components. There are different meanings for the two uses; see
§9.5.3 for details.

Name _____ Datum _____

Rewrite each sentence, making the change indicated in parentheses.

1 Der Schweizer paßt immer gut auf. (future)

_____ Der Schweizer wird immer gut aufpassen. _____

2 Er hat sein Geld in die Unterwäsche eingenäht. (past tense)

----

3 Ich erwarte einen Ausruf des Erstaunens. (perfect verb phrase)

----

4 Die Müllerstochter empfindet Angst. (perfect verb phrase)

----

5 Es fiel ihr auf, daß ... (perfect verb phrase: §7.4.2)

----

6 Der rote Paß der Schweiz wird die Gefahr abwenden. (present)

----

7 Das bedeutet sehr viel. (perfect verb phrase)

----

8 Die Tür ging auf einmal auf. (perfect verb phrase: §7.4.2)

----

9 Ich verspreche dir etwas Schönes. (perfect verb phrase)

----

10 Man verschickt das Chlor in Spezialtankwagen. (future)

----

11 Die Königin bot dem Männchen eine Zigarette an. (perfect
   verb phrase)

----

12 Man zieht dieses Produkt zu Fäden aus. (present passive)

----

13 Weitere Versuche wurden damit angestellt. (past active)

----

14 Chlor hat man zum Bleichen benutzt. (perfect passive)

----

15 Im Jahre 1810 stellte Humphry Davy fest, daß ... (past passive)

Review:

Identify all underlined nouns and pronouns as to whether they are
nominative, accusative, dative, or genitive. Put an "N" above
each nominative, an "A" above each accusative, a "D" above each
dative, and a "G" above each genitive noun or pronoun.

1 Wenn ich ins Ausland gehe, sagt meine Mutter: „Paß auf, daß

  dir nichts gestohlen wird, gib deinen Koffer nicht aus der

  Hand."

2 Schweizer tragen im Ausland ihr Geld in Beuteln unter dem Hemd

  oder eingenäht in die Unterwäsche.

3 Während meines Berlinaufenthaltes passierte ich den Übergang...

Zum Bild der heutigen Schweiz
gehört der Zweite Weltkrieg.

Wer ihn nicht als Erwachsener er-
lebt hat,
hat Mühe, eine politische Meinung
zu vertreten.
Wenn man in einer politischen Dis-
kussion nach dem Jahrgang
gefragt wird,
5 dann aus diesem Grund.
Der Krieg hat unser Selbst-
bewußtsein gestärkt.
Daß wir verschont wurden,
beweist sozusagen alles:
die Kraft unserer Armee,
10 unsere Redlichkeit,
die Stärke des Staates,
die Demokratie
und die Gottgefälligkeit
unseres Landes.
15 Wir Schweizer sind Antikommunisten.
Deshalb bestärkt uns das Erlebnis
des Krieges
in unserem Antikommunismus.
Daß der Krieg gegen die Faschisten
geführt wurde,
ist bedeutungslos geworden.
20 Wir sind überzeugt,

daß es unser Verdienst ist,

verschont worden zu sein,
denn wir müssen mit unserem Ver-
halten, mit unserer Armee und
mit der Schönheit unseres Landes Gott beeindruckt haben.
Wir sind das Land der Freiheit
25 und mit Schiller und den Ausländern
davon überzeugt,
daß wir die Freiheit mit Revolutionen erkämpft hätten.
Das ist nicht wahr.
Wir sind ganz und gar nicht das
Land der Revolutionen
und waren es nie.

An essential part of the picture
of Switzerland today is the
Second World War.
Whoever did not live through it as
an adult
has trouble holding (and defending)
a political opinion.
When during a political discussion
one is asked about his year of
birth,
it is for this reason.
The war strengthened our self-
confidence.
The fact that we were spared
proves everything, so to speak:
the strength of our army,
our integrity,
the strength of the state,
democracy,
and the favor in the eyes of God
of our country.

We Swiss are anti-communists.

Therefore the experience of the war
confirms us
in our anti-communism.
The fact that the war was waged
against the fascists
has become meaningless.
We are convinced
that it is entirely owing to our
efforts
that we were spared,
for we must have made a good impres-
sion on God with our behavior,
with our army, and with the
beauty of our country.
We are the land of freedom,
and, along with Schiller and the
foreigners, convinced
that we have gained freedom by means
of revolutions.
That is not true.
We are not at all the land of revolutions,
and never were.

25 Schiller, Friedrich (1759–1805) –
author of Wilhelm Tell, drama
glorifying the legendary Swiss
hero

NOTES ON LANGUAGE

Be alert to the gender of each noun you encounter. The genders of many nouns are recognizable by their form. §2 of the Grammar Reference Notes has lists of the most common ones.

WORDS AND WORD FAMILIES

erleben (2)
   das Erlebnis/-nisse (16)
die Freiheit -en (24, 26)
heute (adv.)
   heutig- (adj.) (1)
der Krieg -e (6, 16, 18)
   der Weltkrieg (1)

stark
   die Stärke (11)
   stärken (6)
   bestärken (16)
überzeugen (20, 25)
verschonen (7, 22)

COMMENTS ON GRAMMAR

Strong and weak verbs:

The characteristics of the strong verb are:
1) vowel changes to indicate the past tense and, sometimes, the past participle;
2) the ending -en/-n in the past participle.
Some strong verbs have a different vowel in the second and third person singular.
Examples:

Infinitive	(Present 3rd singular)	Past tense	Past participle
riechen		roch	gerochen
nehmen	(nimmt)	nahm	genommen
tragen	(trägt)	trug	getragen
enthalten	(enthält)	enthielt	enthalten

The principal parts of almost all the strong verbs in German are given in §6.2 of the Grammar Reference Notes.

The characteristics of the weak verb are:
1) the ending -te/-ete to indicate the past tense;
2) the ending -t/-et in the past participle.
Some weak verbs (the irregular weak verbs) have a vowel change in the past tense and the past participle. [See §6.1.2.]
Examples:

führen	führte	geführt
eignen	eignete	geeignet
erkämpfen	erkämpfte	erkämpft
protestieren [§9.3.3]	protestierte	protestiert
kennen [§6.1.2]	kannte	gekannt

The principal parts of compound verbs are given as follows:

einnähen	(näht...ein)	nähte...ein	eingenäht
aufpassen	(paßt...auf)	paßte...auf	aufgepaßt
vorkommen	(kommt...vor)	kam...vor	vorgekommen
anfangen	(fängt...an)	fing...an	angefangen

Name _____   Datum _____

All the following verbs are either past tense or past participle
forms. Check to indicate:
    1) whether the verb is weak or strong;
    2) which form each is: past tense or past participle.

	Weak	Strong	Past tense	Past participle
1 erstaunte	✓		✓	
2 befahl		✓	✓	
3 gesponnen				
4 hielt				
5 angefangen				
6 antwortete				
7 geeignet				
8 sprachen				
9 erkundigt				
10 genügten				
11 geschmolzen				
12 ergeben				
13 gefiel				
14 enthalten				
15 bestand				
16 produzierte				
17 abgetötet				
18 verwendeten				
19 benutzt				
20 gestohlen				

Write the nominative singular definite article for each noun in
the list below. [§2]

    1 __die__ Meinung   8 __der__ Antikommunist

    2 _____ Diskussion   9 _____ Faschist

    3 _____ Revolution   10 _____ Schweizer

    4 _____ Redlichkeit   11 _____ Ausländer

    5 _____ Gottgefälligkeit

    6 _____ Schönheit

    7 _____ Freiheit

Aber wir glauben daran,
daß unsere Schweiz eine typische
     Schweiz sei,

und fügen unserem Bild der Schweiz
     kritiklos alles Positive bei,

was Ausländer von der Schweiz
     halten.
5 Wir haben uns angewöhnt,
die Schweiz mit den Augen unserer
     Touristen zu sehen.
Ein Durchschnittsschweizer
hält von der Schweiz genau das-
     selbe
was ein Durchschnittsengländer von
     der Schweiz hält.
10   Unsere Vorstellung von unserem
     Land
ist ein ausländisches Produkt.
Wir leben in der Legende,
die man um uns gemacht hat.
     Unser Land ist 120, vielleicht
     150 Jahre alt.
15 Alles andere ist Vorgeschichte
und hat viel mit unseren Landes-
     grenzen und wenig mit unserem
     Land zu tun.
     Das Wichtigste dieser Vorge-
     schichte
ist das Erringen der Unabhängigkeit.
Unabhängigkeit ist nicht Freiheit,
20 es gibt unabhängige, unfreie Län-
     der.
     Der Schweizer ist überzeugt,
daß nicht der Staat,
sondern die Armee
die Freiheit verteidige und garan-
     tiere.
25 Das ist traurig;
denn die Armee kann nur die Unab-
     hängigkeit verteidigen.
Freiheit ist eine politische Lei-
     stung;
Unabhängigkeit ist zwar ihre Voraus-
     setzung,
aber kein bißchen mehr.
30   In der Geschichte,
die ein Schüler vorgesetzt be-
     kommt,
ist fast nur von militärischen
     Leistungen die Rede;
bestimmt der Einfachheit halber,

denn das Militär vereinfacht alles.

35 Politik ist zu kompliziert,
also lassen wir sie.

But we believe
that our Switzerland is a typical
     Switzerland,
and add uncritically to our picture
     of Switzerland everything posi-
     tive
that foreigners think about Switzer-
     land.
We have become accustomed
to seeing Switzerland with the eyes
     of our tourists.
An average Swiss
has exactly the same opinion about
     Switzerland
as an average Englishman has about
     Switzerland.

     Our idea of our country

is a foreign product.
We live in the legend
that people have made about us.
     Our country is 120, perhaps 150
     years old.
Everything else is prehistory
and has a lot to do with our national
     boundaries and little to do with
     our country.
The most important thing about
     this prehistory
is the gaining of independence.
Independence is not freedom:
there are independent, unfree coun-
     tries.
     The Swiss is convinced
that not the state
but rather the army

defends and guarantees freedom.

That is sad;
for the army can defend only indepen-
     dence.
Freedom is a political accomplish-
     ment;
to be sure, independence is its pre-
     requisite,
but nothing more than that.
     In the history
that a pupil gets put before him (in
     school),
the talk is almost entirely of mili-
     tary accomplishments;
certainly for the sake of simplicity,
for the military simplifies every-
     thing.
Politics is too complicated,
so we leave it alone.

NOTES ON LANGUAGE

3 alles Positive: *Like the neuter
pronouns* etwas *and* nichts *[§5.5.2],*
alles *is often used in combination
with adjectives used as nouns.
However, note that the noun following* etwas *or* nichts *has the neuter
ending* -es, *while the noun following* alles *has the ending* -e.

15 alles andere: *In a similar construction, the word* ander- *is not
capitalized:*
etwas anderes - *something else;*
nichts anderes - *nothing else.*

Subjunctive [§7.6.1]

2 sei
24 verteidige, garantiere: *These
subjunctive forms are used to indicate the author's unwillingness
to take responsibility for the
statements.*

Prepositions

1 glauben (an + *acc.*) - *believe (in)*
4 halten (von) - *think (of), consider, regard*

WORDS AND WORD FAMILIES

der Ausländer - (4)
    ausländisch (11)
der Durchschnitt:
    der Durchschnittsengländer (9)
    der Durchschnittsschweizer (7)
einfach:
    die Einfachheit (33)
    vereinfachen (34)

die Geschichte (30)
    die Vorgeschichte (15, 17)
halten [7a] (von) (4, 8, 9)
die Leistung -en (27, 32)
sondern (23)
unabhängig (20)
    die Unabhängigkeit (18, 19, 26)
verteidigen (24, 26)

COMMENTS ON GRAMMAR

Descriptive adjectives:

An adjective which modifies a <u>following</u> noun is a descriptive adjective. Descriptive adjectives have endings. These endings are shown in the tables in §4.5, §4.6, and §4.7. Examples:

> ein gar zu <u>lächerliches</u> Männchen
> der <u>elastische</u> Faden
> <u>unabhängige</u>, <u>unfreie</u> Länder

Predicate adjectives:

A predicate adjective is an adjective that modifies the subject but stands after the verb. Predicate adjectives have no ending. Examples:

> Das Männchen ist gar zu <u>lächerlich</u>.
> Der Faden wird <u>elastisch</u>.
> Diese Länder sind <u>unabhängig</u> aber <u>unfrei</u>.

Adverbs that modify verbs:

Adverbs have the form of an adjective without an ending. They have a function like many English adverbs that consist of adjective + -ly, like "quickly, painfully." Examples:

> Sie tragen ihren Paß <u>unauffällig</u> *(inconspicuously)* in der Hand.
> Heute wird Chlor <u>billig</u> *(cheaply)* aus Kochsalzlösung gewonnen.

Adverbs that modify adjectives:

Some constructions are "three layers deep." On the top layer is a noun:

> Die Baumwolle hat <u>Fasern</u>.

The second layer consists of an adjective or adjectives modifying the noun; such adjectives of course have the regular adjective endings:

> Die Baumwolle hat <u>zerreißbare</u> Fasern.

On the third level is an adverb modifying an adjective; such an adverb has no ending:

> Die Baumwolle hat <u>leicht</u> zerreißbare Fasern.

Note the difference between the two examples:

> die <u>typisch</u> schweizerische Legende *(the typically Swiss legend)*
> die <u>typische</u> schweizerische Legende *(the typical Swiss legend)*

Comparative forms [§4.8]:

The marker for adjectives in the "comparative degree" is -er. It signals a meaning like that of English "quicker, better, more intelligent." The comparative stem ends in -er, which is followed by an appropriate ending when it is used as a descriptive adjective:

> eine reichere Frau

When used as adverbs or predicate adjectives, comparative forms have only the ending -er and no descriptive adjective ending:

> leichter zerreißbare Fasern
> Sein Herz wurde noch goldgieriger.

Often a comparative adjective or adverb is used with als in the meaning "than." [§18.1.3]

> Etwas Lebendes ist mir lieber als alle Schätze der Welt.

Superlative forms [§4.8]

The marker for adjectives in the "superlative degree" is -(e)st-. It signals a meaning like that of English "quickest, best, most intelligent." The superlative stem ends in -(e)st-, which is followed by an appropriate ending.

> In den meisten Trinkwasseranlagen wird Chlor benutzt.
> die ungewöhnlichsten und seltsamsten Namen

A superlative adverb normally has the formula: am ...sten.

> Dann schmeckt es am salzigsten.
> So wird Chlor am billigsten gewonnen.

Name _____ Datum _____

Referring to §4.1-7 when necessary, write the appropriate descriptive-adjective, predicate-adjective, or adverb form of the word in parentheses in the blank provided. Then translate the entire sentence into English.

1 Die Schweizer haben ein ___kritikloses___ Bild der Schweiz. (kritiklos)

_____*The Swiss have an uncritical view of Switzerland.*_____

2 Die _____ Touristen sind die Engländer. (wichtigst-)

----

3 Wir haben eine _____ Vorstellung von unserem Land. (positiv)

----

4 Ein unabhängiges Land kann _____ sein. (unfrei)

----

5 Es ist eine _____ Tatsache, daß viele Länder unfrei sind. (traurig)

----

6 Es gibt _____ und _____ Leistungen in unserer Geschichte. (politisch, militärisch)

----

7 Unabhängigkeit ist die Voraussetzung der _____ Freiheit. (politisch)

----

8 Unter Hitler war Deutschland ein _____ unfreies Land. (politisch)

----

9 Der _____ Paß der Schweiz hat ein _____
  Kreuz. (rot, weiß)

  ----

10 Während meines _____ Berlinaufenthaltes passierte ich oft den Grenzübergang. (letzt)

Review:

Write the nominative singular definite article for each noun in
the list below. [§2]

1 _____ Unabhängigkeit		11 _____ Tourist
2 _____ Einfachheit		12 _____ Engländer
3 _____ Vorstellung		
4 _____ Leistung		13 _____ Erringen [§2.5]
5 _____ Voraussetzung		
6 _____ Überzeugung		
7 _____ Legende		
8 _____ Geschichte		
9 _____ Grenze		
10 _____ Rede		

Ich lebe in diesem Land.
Es läßt sich in diesem Land
    leben.
Ich bin hier geboren.
Ich bin hier aufgewachsen.
5 Ich verstehe die Sprache dieser
    Gegend.
    Ich fühle mich hier zu Hause.
Auch mir fällt es schwer,
mir vorzustellen,
daß sich jemand so zu Hause fühlen
    kann,
10 wie ein Schweizer in der Schweiz.
    Die Schweiz ist mir bekannt.
Das macht sie mir angenehm.
Hier kenne ich die Organisation.
Hier kann ich etwas durchschauen.
15 Ich weiß,
wieviel hier die Dinge ungefähr
    kosten,
und ich brauche das Geld, mit dem
    ich bezahle, nicht umzu-
    rechnen.
    Ich liebe diese Gegend,
und es ist mir wichtig,
20 Bürger dieses Landes zu sein,
weil mir mein Bürgerrecht garan-
    tiert,
daß ich unter allen Umständen hier
    bleiben darf.
    Ich habe das Recht,
hier zu bleiben.
25 Das ist mir viel wert.
Es macht mir auch Spaß,
und ich werde bleiben,
dem Satze zum Trotz:
„Du kannst ja gehen,
30 wenn es dir hier nicht paßt!"
    Doch möchte ich hier leben
    dürfen,
ohne ständig begeistert sein zu
    müssen.
Ich bin nicht als Tourist hier.
Was mich freut
35 und was mir Spaß macht,
was mich beschäftigt,
hat fast ausschließlich mit der
    Schweiz und mit Schweizern
    zu tun.
Das meine ich, wenn ich sage:
„Ich bin Schweizer."

— Peter Bichsel

I live in this country.
This is a good country to live
    in.
I was born here.
I grew up here.
I understand the language of this
    region.
    I feel at home here.
*It **is** hard for me, too,*
to imagine

that anyone can feel as much at home

as a Swiss in Switzerland.
    I know Switzerland.
That makes it pleasant for me.
I know the way things are done here.
I understand the reason for things.
I know
approximately how much things cost
    here,
and I don't need to figure the ex-
    change rate for the money with
    which I pay.
    I love this region,
and it is important to me
to be a citizen of this country,
because my right as a citizen guaran-
    tees me
that I am permitted to stay here
    under any circumstances.
    I have the right
to stay here.
That is worth a great deal to me.
It amuses me, too,
and I want to remain
in spite of the saying,
"You can leave, you know,
if it doesn't suit you here!"
    However, I'd like to be allowed
    to live here
without having to be constantly en-
    thusiastic.
I am not here as a tourist.
What makes me happy,
and what amuses me,
what keeps me occupied,

has to do almost exclusively with
    Switzerland and the Swiss.

That's what I mean when I say,
"I am a Swiss."

NOTES ON LANGUAGE

Note the following useful expressions. In parentheses are common words that can be used to vary these expressions.

6 sich (zu Hause) (wohl) fühlen – *feel (at home) (well)*

7 es fällt mir (nicht) (sehr) schwer – *it is (not) (very) hard for me*

8 sich etwas vorstellen – *imagine something*

11 es ist mir bekannt – *I am acquainted with it*

12 es ist mir angenehm – *it is pleasant for me*

19 es ist mir (nicht) (sehr) wichtig – *it is (not) (very) important to me*

25 es ist mir (nicht) (viel) wert – *it is (not) worth (much) to me*

26 es macht mir (viel) (nicht viel) (keinen) Spaß – *it is (a lot of) (not much) (no) fun for me*

30 es paßt mir (paßt mir nicht) – *it suits me (doesn't suit me)*

32 ohne...zu + *infinitive* – *without ----ing ...*

34 es freut mich (sehr) – *I am (very) glad*

WORDS AND WORD FAMILIES

angenehm sein (+ *dat.*) (12)
bekannt sein (+ *dat.*) (11)
der Bürger – (20)
   das Bürgerrecht -e (21)
freuen (+ *acc.*) (34)
sich (*acc.*) fühlen (6, 9)
ohne ... zu (+ *infinitive*)   (32)
passen (+ *dat.*)   (30)

das Recht -e (23)
   das Bürgerrecht (21)
schwer fallen (+ *dat.*) (7)
Spaß machen (+ *dat.*)   (26, 35)
sich (*dat.*) etwas (*acc.*)
   vor·stellen (8)
wert sein (+ *dat.*)   (25)
wichtig sein (+ *dat.*)   (19)

COMMENTS ON GRAMMAR

Modal auxiliaries:

Six extremely important, extremely irregular verbs are called "modal auxiliaries." These are: **dürfen, können, mögen, müssen, sollen, wollen.** The present-tense forms and the past-tense stems of these verbs appear on page 12. Their principal parts are in §6.1.3 of the Grammar Reference Notes.

The modals have a very wide range of meanings. See §7.8.2 for some of the most important.

Normally a modal is used with the infinitive of a main verb. This infinitive is <u>not</u> preceded by **zu.** Compare the following pairs of sentences, with and without a modal.

Without a modal:	With a modal:
Present: Die Armee verteidigt nur die Unabhängigkeit.	Die Armee kann nur die Unabhängigkeit verteidigen.
Past: Ich ging ins Ausland.	Ich wollte ins Ausland gehen.

A special construction is a perfect verb phrase with a modal. Such constructions have the formula: inflected form of the perfect auxiliary **haben** + ... + main verb infinitive + modal auxiliary infinitive. The infinitives of the main verb and the modal are called a "double infinitive."

Perfect verb phrase:	
Der Tourist hat oft den Grenzübergang passiert.	Der Tourist hat oft den Grenzübergang passieren müssen.
Bichsel <u>ist</u> in der Schweiz geblieben.	Bichsel <u>hat</u> in der Schweiz bleiben wollen.

In subordinate clauses the end elements are in the order: ... inflected form of **haben** + double infinitive.

Wir wissen schon, daß Bichsel in der Schweiz geblieben ist.	Wir wissen schon, daß Bichsel in der Schweiz hat bleiben wollen.

The future verb phrase has a double infinitive, which is used with the future auxiliary **werden.**

Future verb phrase:	
Der Tourist wird oft den Grenzübergang passieren.	Der Tourist wird oft den Grenzübergang passieren müssen.

Compare the following sentences, which illustrate the passive verb phrase with and without a modal:

Present passive verb phrase:	
Chlor wird in den Trinkwasseranlagen benutzt.	Chlor kann in den Trinkwasseranlagen benutzt werden.
Past passive verb phrase:	
Die Schweizer wurden verschont.	Die Schweizer wollten verschont werden.

Rarely, a perfect construction has a modal auxiliary without a dependent infinitive. In such constructions the modal has an ordinary weak past participle.

> Nur Karl hat nicht gewollt.
> Vor vierzig Jahren habe ich gut Französisch gekonnt.

Name _____ Datum _____

Rewrite each sentence, using the modal given. Keep the corresponding tense or verb phrase.

1 In der Schweiz bezahlt man immer mit schweizerischem Geld. (können)

_____ In der Schweiz kann man immer mit schweizerischem Geld bezahlen. _____

2 Der Tourist war ständig begeistert. (müssen)

_____ Der Tourist mußte ständig begeistert sein. _____

3 Peter Bichsel bleibt unter allen Umständen in der Schweiz. (wollen)

_____

_____

4 Sein Bürgerrecht garantiert ihm das. (sollen)

_____

5 Die Dinge kosten hier zu viel. (sollen)

_____

6 Das meine ich! (wollen)

_____

7 Das ist wahr. (mögen)

_____

8 Der Staat verteidigt und garantiert die Freiheit. (müssen)

_____

_____

9 Die Königin gab dem Männlein ihr Kind nicht. (wollen)

_____

_____

10 Der rote Paß der Schweiz wird die Gefahr abwenden. (können)

_____

_____

11 Der Krieg wurde gegen die Faschisten geführt. (müssen)

_____

12 Im Jahre 1810 wurde festgestellt, daß ... (können)

----

13 Wir haben uns hier nie zu Hause gefühlt. (können)

----

14 Der Reisende hat sein Geld in die Unterwäsche eingenäht.
   (müssen)

----

15 Die Ausländer sind nicht in der Schweiz geblieben. (dürfen)

BIOLOGIE

WAS SÄUGETIERE FRESSEN

WHAT MAMMALS EAT

Manche Säugetiere ernähren sich
nur von pflanzlicher Kost,
manche fressen nur andere Tiere
und manche nehmen regelmäßig sowohl
    pflanzliche als auch fleisch-
    liche Nahrung auf.
5 Wir unterscheiden
Pflanzenfresser,
Fleischfresser
und Allesfresser.
    Allerdings sind auch die Pflan-
    zenfresser und Fleischfresser
    nicht ganz streng zu trennen.
10 Manche Pflanzenfresser ernähren
    sich
häufig nebenher von Kleintieren.

Manche Fleischfresser
nehmen auch Beeren, andere Früchte
    oder junge Triebe auf.
    Manche Pflanzenfresser ernähren
    sich
15 ziemlich wahllos
von Blättern, Gräsern, Früchten
    usw.
Andere sind auf bestimmte Pflanzen-
    kost (beispielsweise Sämerei-
    en) angewiesen.
Ähnliches ist auch bei Fleisch-
    fressern zu beobachten.
Manche fressen alle Tiere,
20 die sie überwältigen können.
Andere haben sich auf einen bestimm-
    ten Nahrungserwerb (zum Bei-
    spiel auf den Fischfang oder
    auf das Fressen von Schlangen)
    spezialisiert.
    Pflanzenfresser werden größer
    und schwerer als Fleischfres-
    ser.
Von den Landsäugetieren
    ist der Eisbär der größte Fleisch-
    fresser
25 und der Elefant der größte Pflan-
    zenfresser.
In unserer Heimat
    ist die Wildkatze der größte
        Fleischfresser
    (bis 11 kg schwer)
und der Rothirsch der größte
    Pflanzenfresser
30 (bis 200 kg schwer).
    Fleischfresser sind meist in
        ihren Bewegungen viel gewandter
als Pflanzenfresser.
Sie können oft schneller laufen

Some mammals feed (subsist)
only on plant food,
some eat only other animals,

and some regularly accept both plant
    food and meat.

We make a distinction among
herbivores,
carnivores,
and omnivores.
    To be sure, even the herbivores
    and carnivores cannot be
    strictly divided.

Some herbivores feed
frequently on small animals in addi-
    tion (to their usual fare).
Some carnivores
also eat berries, other fruits, or
    young shoots.

    Some herbivores feed

rather indiscriminately

on leaves, grasses, fruits, etc.

Others are dependent on certain plant
    food (for example, seeds).

Something similar can also be ob-
    served in carnivores.
Some eat all the animals
which they can overpower.

Others have specialized in acquiring
    a certain food (for example, in
    catching fish or eating snakes).

    Herbivores get bigger and heavier
    than carnivores.

Of the land mammals
the polar bear is the biggest carni-
    vore,
and the elephant the biggest herbi-
    vore.
In our homeland (East Germany)

the wildcat is the biggest carnivore

(up to 11 kilograms in weight),
and the red deer (stag) the biggest
    herbivore
(up to 200 kilograms).
    Carnivores are usually much more
    agile in their movements
than herbivores.
They can often run faster

und besser springen und klettern.	and jump and climb better.
35 Außerdem haben sie besonders gut funktionierende Sinnesorgane	Moreover, they have sense-organs that function especially well
(besonders die Augen und die Nase).	(especially the eyes and the nose).
Beides zusammen	The two together
ist ihnen beim Erbeuten der Nahrungstiere von großem Nutzen.	are of great use to them in the capturing of prey.
In einem Gebiet	In any one region
40 leben stets viel mehr	there always live many more
Pflanzen- als Fleischfresser.	herbi(vores) than carnivores.
Ein Löwe reißt	A lion seizes (tears up)
im Jahr etwa 50 Zebras.	about 50 zebras a year.
In seinem Wohngebiet	In his range,
45 müssen also mindestens 50 Zebras genügend Nahrung finden.	therefore, at least 50 zebras must find sufficient food.
Das ist mit	That is also
eine Ursache dafür,	a reason for the fact
daß Fleischfresser einzeln oder in kleinen Rudeln, Pflanzenfresser aber oft in großen Herden leben.	that carnivores live alone or in small packs, whereas herbivores often live in large herds.

NOTES ON LANGUAGE

4 sowohl ... als auch - ... *as well as..., both ... and ...*

9 sind ... zu trennen [§7.5.3] - *can be separated*

18 ist ... zu beobachten - *can be observed*

37 Beides zusammen ist ...: *Singular in form (with a singular verb), plural in meaning.*

46-47 Das ist mit / eine Ursache...: *Obviously* mit *cannot be a preposition here, because the noun following it is not in the dative. Consult your dictionary for the entries under "mit."*

Cultural note:
essen, trinken: *used with human beings*
fressen, saufen: *applied to lower animals*
    There are a number of such words, which are normally used only with animals. They have a pejorative meaning when applied to human beings. Saufen, when applied to humans, means: drink too much alcohol. Examples:
Friß nicht wie ein Schwein!
Er säuft sich dumm.

WORDS AND WORD FAMILIES

auf·nehmen [5c]   (4, 13)
bestimmt *(adj.)*   (17, 21)
fressen [4a]   (3, 19, 21)
die Frucht/Früchte (13, 16)
das Gebiet -e (39)
    das Wohngebiet (44)
die Kost (2)
    die Pflanzenkost (17)

die Nahrung (4, 45)
    sich ernähren (1, 10, 14)
    das Nahrungstier (38)
sowohl ... als auch (4)
das Tier -e (19)
    das Säugetier (1)
    das Kleintier (11)
    das Landsäugetier (23)

COMMENTS ON GRAMMAR

Expressions with passive meaning:

   The passive meaning involves a focus upon a process itself,
and shifts attention away from the performer of the process.
German has several grammatical formulas to express this desired
distribution of emphasis.

1) **werden** + past participle (discussed more fully on page 39)
   Examples:

      Chlor wird benutzt, um Bakterien abzutöten. *(is used)*
      Paß auf, daß dir nichts gestohlen wird. *(is stolen)*

2) **man** + 3rd person singular inflected verb.
   Examples:

      Man nennt dieses Verfahren Elektrolyse. *(is called)*
      Man erhielt ein Produkt. *(was obtained)*

3) nominative (referring to an inanimate thing) + inflected verb
   + **sich**.
   Examples:

      Stroh spinnt sich normalerweise nicht zu Gold. *(straw is spun)*
      Durch Abkühlung und durch Druck verwandelt sich Chlorgas in Flüssig-
         keit. *(chlorine gas is changed)*

4) **sein** + **zu** + infinitive.
   Examples:

      Die Pflanzenfresser und Fleischfresser sind nicht ganz streng zu
         trennen. *(can be separated)*
      Ähnliches ist auch bei Fleischfressern zu beobachten. *(can be observed)*

5) **lassen** + **sich** + infinitive.
   Examples:

      Dieses Produkt ließ sich zu Fäden ausziehen. *(could be drawn out)*
      Die Fäden lassen sich noch weiter strecken. *(can be stretched)*

Imperatives:

   The imperative forms are used in suggestions, requests, in-
structions, orders, commands.
   Since an imperative is addressed to someone, there are as
many imperative forms as there are second-person pronouns:
du, ihr, Sie.
Examples:

du	ihr	Sie
Paß auf!	Paßt auf!	Passen Sie auf!
Gib deinen Koffer nicht aus der Hand!	Gebt euren Koffer nicht aus der Hand!	Geben Sie Ihren Koffer nicht aus der Hand!
Sei nicht so gold-gierig!	Seid nicht so gold-gierig!	Seien Sie nicht so gold-gierig!
Stell dir vor, wieviel das kosten wird!	Stellt euch vor, wieviel das kosten wird!	Stellen Sie sich vor, wie-viel das kosten wird!
Fahr langsamer!	Fahrt langsamer!	Fahren Sie langsamer!

The singular imperative (**du**-form) has the ending **-e** in older German, usually no ending in more modern German.

Strong verbs which have the vowel **i** or **ie** in the second and third person singular present have that vowel also in the singular imperative.
Examples:

Gib!	Gebt!	Geben Sie!
Iß!	Eßt!	Essen Sie!
Nimm!	Nehmt!	Nehmen Sie!
Sieh!	Seht!	Sehen Sie!

A first-person plural imperative has a meaning like English "Let's."
Examples:

> Passen wir hier auf!
> Gehen wir nach Hause!
> Fahren wir langsamer!

The separable component of a compound verb is separated from the root verb and is at the end of the clause:

> Schließen Sie, bitte, den Koffer zu!
> Fangen wir an!

Imperatives in German are punctuated with an exclamation mark.

Name _____ Datum _____

Rewrite each of the following two sentences, using the alternative passive formulations:
   a) lassen + sich + infinitive;
   b) können + past participle + werden;
   c) man + kann + infinitive.

1 Die Pflanzenfresser und Fleischfresser sind nicht ganz streng
  zu trennen.

   a) _____

   _____

   b) _____

   _____

   c) _____

   _____

2 Ähnliches ist bei Fleischfressern zu beobachten.

   a) _____

   _____

   b) _____

   _____

   c) _____

   _____

Using the vocabulary given, make the four possible imperatives:
a) du; b) ihr; c) Sie; d) wir.

1 laufen - schneller

   a) __Lauf schneller!_____   b) __Lauft schneller!_____

   c) __Laufen Sie schneller!_____   d) __Laufen wir schneller!_____

2 nehmen - diesen Ring

   a) _____

   b) _____

   c) _____

   d) _____

3 anfangen - in dieser Nacht

   a) _____

   b) _____

   c) _____

   d) _____

4 sich hinsetzen - hier

   a) _____

   b) _____

   c) _____

   d) _____

5 essen - nicht so viel

   a) _____

   b) _____

   c) _____

   d) _____

DAS GEBISS DER PFLANZENFRESSER

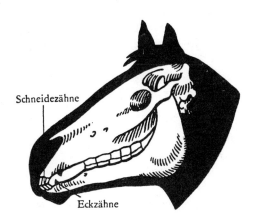

Mit seinen Nagezähnen zerkleinert der Hase harte Pflanzenstoffe. Durch mahlende Bewegungen beider Kiefer wird die Nahrung zwischen den Backenzähnen zerrieben. Die Nagezähne wachsen zeitlebens von unten nach und werden durch dauerndes Nagen scharf gehalten. Ratten zerstören mit diesem Nagen sogar Mauerwerk und dicke Bleirohre. Bricht ein Nagezahn ab, wächst der gegenüberstehende krankhaft weiter.

Beim Pferd sind statt der Nagezähne Schneidezähne ausgebildet. Sie sind schräg nach vorn gerichtet und stumpf, passen aber sehr genau aufeinander. Dadurch eignen sie sich gut zum Abreißen von Gräsern. Die abgerupfte Nahrung wird zwischen den Backenzähnen zerrieben. Sie haben sehr breite Kauflächen und passen ebenfalls gut aufeinander. In der Lücke zwischen den Schneide- und Backenzähnen stehen Eckzähne.

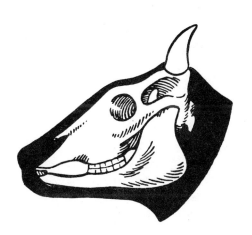

Das Hausrind frißt die gleichen Pflanzenstoffe wie das Pferd. Sein Gebiß ist jedoch ganz anders gebaut. Im Oberkiefer sind überhaupt keine Schneidezähne und Eckzähne ausgebildet. Im Unterkiefer sind diese Zähne nur noch verkümmert vorhanden und taugen nicht zum Abbeißen von Gräsern. Diese Gräser werden von der Kuh auch mit dem breiten Maul und der auffällig langen Zunge abgerupft. Die Backenzähne zermahlen sie dann.

DAS GEBISS DER PFLANZENFRESSER

Mit seinen Nagezähnen
zerkleinert der Hase
harte Pflanzenstoffe.
Durch mahlende Bewegungen beider
Kiefer
5 wird die Nahrung zwischen den
Backenzähnen zerrieben.
Die Nagezähne wachsen zeitlebens
von unten nach
und werden durch dauerndes Nagen
scharf gehalten.
Ratten zerstören mit diesem Nagen
sogar Mauerwerk und dicke Bleirohre.
10 Bricht ein Nagezahn ab,
wächst der gegenüberstehende krankhaft weiter.
Beim Pferd sind
statt der Nagezähne
Schneidezähne
15 ausgebildet.
Sie sind schräg nach vorn gerichtet
und stumpf,

passen aber sehr genau aufeinander.

Dadurch eignen sie sich gut
20 zum Abreißen von Gräsern.
Die abgerupfte Nahrung
wird zwischen den Backenzähnen
(Mahlzähnen) zerrieben.
Sie haben sehr breite Kauflächen
und passen ebenfalls gut aufeinander.
25 In der Lücke
zwischen den Schneidezähnen und
Backenzähnen
stehen Eckzähne.
Das Hausrind
frißt die gleichen Pflanzenstoffe
30 wie das Pferd.
Sein Gebiß

ist jedoch ganz anders gebaut.

Im Oberkiefer
sind überhaupt keine Schneidezähne
und Eckzähne ausgebildet.
35 Im Unterkiefer
sind diese Zähne nur noch verkümmert vorhanden
und taugen nicht zum Abbeißen von
Gräsern.

THE TEETH OF HERBIVORES

With his gnawing teeth
the hare grinds up
hard plant materials.
By means of grinding motions of both
jaws
the food is ground up between the
molars (cheek teeth).
The gnawing teeth keep growing from
below throughout life
and are kept sharp by means of con-
stant gnawing.
Rats destroy with this gnawing

even masonry and thick lead pipes.

If a gnawing tooth breaks off,
the one opposite keeps on growing
pathologically.
In the case of the horse,
instead of the gnawing teeth,
incisors
(are) developed.
They are aligned on a forward slope
and blunt;
however, they fit exactly on one
another.
Because of this they are well suited
for tearing off grasses.
The plucked-off food

is ground up between the molars.

They have very broad chewing surfaces

and also fit well on one another.

In the space

between the incisors and molars

are canine teeth.
The domestic bovine
eats the same plant materials
as the horse.
Its dentition
is, however, constructed completely
differently.
In the upper jaw
no incisors and no canines at all
are developed.
In the lower jaw
these teeth are almost completely
atrophied
and are worthless for biting off
grasses.

Diese Gräser
werden von der Kuh auch mit dem
    breiten Maul und der auffällig
    langen Zunge abgerupft.
40 Die Backenzähne
zermahlen sie dann.

These grasses
are plucked off by the cow, with her
*   broad mouth and her conspicuous-*
*   ly long tongue.*
The molars
then grind them up.

NOTES ON LANGUAGE

9 Bricht ein Nagezahn ab,... = Wenn
ein Nagezahn abbricht,...

Notice that the prefix zer- usual-
ly adds the meaning "all to pieces:"
zerreißen [1b] - *tear to pieces.*
Examples:
2 zerkleinert
5 zerrieben
8 zerstören
41 zermahlen

Notice the difference between:
1) The sentences with sein + *past*
*   participle, describing a state:*
12 Beim Pferd <u>sind</u>...Schneidezähne
<u>ausgebildet</u>
16 ...sind...gerichtet.
32 ... ist...gebaut.

2) The sentences with werden +
*   past participle, describing a*
*   process:*
5 Die Nahrung <u>wird</u> zwischen den
Backenzähnen <u>zerrieben</u>.
7 ...werden...gehalten.
39 ...werden...abgerupft.

WORDS AND WORD FAMILIES

aus·bilden (15, 34)
beißen [1b]
   ab·beißen (37)
   das Gebiß/-bisse (31)
das Gras/Gräser (20, 37, 38)
der Kiefer - (4)
   der Oberkiefer (33)
   der Unterkiefer (35)

mahlen (4)
   der Mahlzahn/-zähne (22)
   zermahlen (41)
nagen (7, 8)
   der Nagezahn/-zähne (1, 6)
passen (18, 24)
das Pferd -e (12, 30)
zerstören (8)

COMMENTS ON GRAMMAR

The past participle:

    Sometimes the past participle is used as an adjective, with the appropriate adjective ending.
Examples:

              die abgerupfte Nahrung
              geschmolzener Zucker
              diese hindurchgepreßte Flüssigkeit

The present participle:

    The present participle is derived from the infinitive by the addition of **-d**.
Examples:

              mahlend   *(grinding)*
              dauernd   *(persisting)*
              gegenüberstehend   *(standing opposite)*

    The present participle is sometimes used as an adjective, with the appropriate adjective ending.
Examples:

        ... die <u>mahlenden</u> Bewegungen beider Kiefer.
        Sie werden durch <u>dauerndes</u> Nagen scharf gehalten.
        Fleischfresser haben besonders gut <u>funktionierende</u> Sinnes-
        organe.
        ... ein übel <u>riechendes</u> Gas.

    Both the past and the present participle may be used without an ending, as a predicate adjective or, adverbially, as the modifier of a verb or another adjective.
Examples:

Past participle: Bei Kühen und Pferden sind im Oberkiefer keine Schneide-
                  oder Eckzähne <u>ausgebildet</u>.
                Im Unterkiefer sind diese Zähne nur noch <u>verkümmert</u>
                vorhanden.
Present participle: Sie traten <u>lachend</u> herein.
        ... ein <u>erstickend</u> riechendes Gas.

Name _____ Datum _____

From the infinitive given in parentheses, form the past participle and write it with its appropriate ending in the blank provided.

1 Die ____beobachteten____ Fleischfresser waren kleiner als die Pflanzenfresser. (beobachten)

2 Unter den _____ Früchten waren viele Beeren. (aufnehmen)

3 Von Fleischfressern werden oft auch junge Triebe _____. (fressen)

4 Bichsel kann sein _____ Bürgerrecht nicht verlieren. (garantieren)

5 Die _____ Unabhängigkeit ist ein wichtiger Teil unserer Geschichte. (erringen [3a])

6 Das aus Kochsalzlösung _____ Chlor ist billig. (gewinnen [3b])

7 Die Schweizer sind _____ Antikommunisten. (überzeugen)

8 Die _____ Bakterien sind uns nicht mehr schädlich. (abtöten)

9 Nylon wurde 1938 in den _____ Staaten auf den Markt gebracht. (vereinigen)

10 Nun gib mir, was du _____ hast. (versprechen)

From the infinitive given in parentheses, form the present participle and write it with its appropriate ending in the blank provided.

1 Der ____hereintretende____ König fand alles, wie er es gewünscht hatte. (hereintreten)

2 Kochsalz ist eine Verbindung von zwei häufig _____ Elementen. (vorkommen)

3 Schweiß ist ein salzig _____ Sekret des menschlichen Körpers. (schmecken)   (das Sekret)

4 Ein _____ Schweizer gibt seinen Koffer
nicht aus der Hand. (aufpassen)

5 Das _____ Männlein stieß mit dem Fuß
tief in die Erde. (schreien)

Review:

Give the nominative singular definite article for each noun in
the list below.

1 _____ Abbeißen

2 _____ Abreißen

3 _____ Bewegung

4 _____ Kaufläche

5 _____ Lücke

6 _____ Nagen

7 _____ Nahrung

8 _____ Ratte

9 _____ Zunge

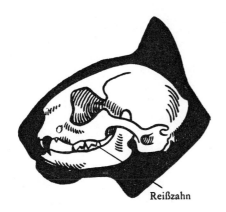

Reißzahn

Bei der Katze dienen die Zähne kaum noch zum Kauen, sondern mehr zum Packen und Zerreißen der Beute sowie als Waffe im Kampf. Auffällig groß sind die Eckzähne, mit denen die Beute gepackt und festgehalten wird. Auch die Backenzähne haben keine Mahlflächen, sondern messerscharfe Kanten und Zacken zum Zerteilen der Beute und zum Zerknacken von Knochen. Die hintersten, größten Backenzähne heißen Reißzähne.

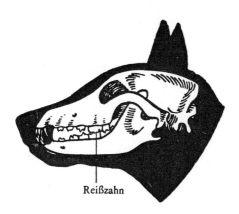

Reißzahn

Der Hund hat ein anders gebautes Gebiß als die Katze. Seine Eckzähne sind kleiner. Hinter den Reißzähnen sind weitere Backenzähne vorhanden, die Mahlflächen besitzen und noch zum richtigen Kauen verwendet werden können. Die vorderen Backenzähne arbeiten ebenso wie bei der Katze. Die Schneidezähne sind größer als bei der Katze, stehen in einer Reihe nebeneinander und dienen hauptsächlich zum Abnagen von Knochen.

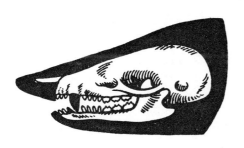

Auch der unterirdisch lebende Maulwurf ist ein Fleischfresser. Seine Nahrung besteht aus Kleintieren. Das Gebiß ist zum Zerbeißen harter Insekten-Panzer eingerichtet. Alle Zähne sind messerscharf, dolchförmig oder mit spitzen Zacken und Höckern versehen. Ein ebensolches Gebiß haben auch die Spitzmäuse. Am Fehlen der typischen Nagezähne kann man diese nützlichen Tiere leicht von den echten Mäusen unterscheiden.

DAS GEBISS DER FLEISCHFRESSER

    Bei der Katze
dienen die Zähne kaum noch zum
    Kauen,
sondern mehr zum Packen
und Zerreißen der Beute
5 sowie
als Waffe im Kampf.
Auffällig groß sind die Eckzähne,
mit denen die Beute gepackt und
    festgehalten wird.
Auch die Backenzähne haben keine
    Mahlflächen
10 sondern messerscharfe Kanten und
    Zacken
zum Zerteilen der Beute
und zum Zerknacken von Knochen.
Die hintersten, größten Backen-
    zähne
heißen Reißzähne.
15   Der Hund hat ein anders gebau-
    tes Gebiß
als die Katze.
Hinter den Reißzähnen
sind weitere Backenzähne vorhanden,
die Mahlflächen besitzen
20 und noch zum richtigen Kauen ver-
    wendet werden können.
Die vorderen Backenzähne arbeiten
ebenso wie
bei der Katze.
Die Schneidezähne sind größer als
    bei der Katze,
25 stehen in einer Reihe nebenein-
    ander
und dienen hauptsächlich
zum Abnagen von Knochen.
    Auch der unterirdisch lebende
    Maulwurf
ist ein Fleischfresser.
30 Seine Nahrung
besteht aus Kleintieren.
Das Gebiß
ist zum Zerbeißen harter Insekten-
    Panzer eingerichtet.
Alle Zähne sind messerscharf,
35 dolchförmig
oder mit spitzen Zacken und Höckern
    versehen.
Ein ebensolches Gebiß haben auch
    die Spitzmäuse.

Am Fehlen der typischen Nagezähne

kann man diese nützlichen Tiere
    leicht von den echten Mäusen
    unterscheiden.

THE TEETH OF CARNIVORES

    In the case of the cat,

the teeth hardly serve for chewing,

but rather for the seizing
and tearing apart of prey,
and also
as a weapon in a fight.
Conspicuously large are the canines,
with which the prey is seized and
    held fast.
Moreover, the molars have no grind-
    ing surfaces,
but rather knife-sharp edges and
    points
for the splitting up of prey
and for the cracking up of bones.

The hindmost, biggest cheek-teeth

are called carnassial teeth.
    The dog has a differently con-
    structed set of teeth
from the cat.
Behind the carnassial teeth
there are additional cheek-teeth,
which have grinding surfaces

and can be used for actual chewing.

The molars in front of them work
just as (they do)
in the cat.
The incisors are bigger than (they
    are) in the cat;
they stand in a row next to each
    other
and serve mainly
for the gnawing of bones.
    Also the mole, which lives under-
    ground,
is a carnivore.
Its food
consists of small animals.
The dentition
is arranged for the crunching of
    hard insect shells (armor).
All the teeth are sharp as knives,
dagger-shaped,
or provided with sharp points and
    humps.
Shrews, too, have exactly the same
    kind of teeth.
By the lack of the typical gnawing
    teeth

one can easily differentiate these
    useful animals from real mice.

NOTES ON LANGUAGE

Compounds:
Several of the possible combinations are exemplified in this passage:

Title: der Fleischfresser (das Fleisch + der Fresser)

7 der Eckzahn (die Ecke - -e + der Zahn)

9 der Backenzahn (die Backe + -n + der Zahn)

9 die Mahlfläche (mahlen - -en + die Fläche)

10 messerscharf (das Messer + scharf)

14 der Reißzahn (reißen - -en + der Zahn)

24 der Schneidezahn (schneiden - -n + der Zahn)

28 unterirdisch (unter + die Erde - -e + -isch — *the initial* e *of* Erde > i *with the addition of the adjective-forming ending* -isch.)

31 das Kleintier (klein + das Tier)

35 dolchförmig (der Dolch + die Form + ̈ig — *the* o *of* Form *has Umlaut when the adjective-forming ending* -ig *is added.)*

Note that the entire compound takes on the characteristics of the final segment:
1) the gender of the compound noun is determined by the gender of the last noun;
2) if the last segment is adjectival, the word is not capitalized, even though its first segment may be a noun.

WORDS AND WORD FAMILIES

die Beute (4, 8, 11)
bestehen [§6.2.2] (aus)   (31)
dienen (2, 26)
die Fläche -n
   die Mahlfläche (9, 19)

kauen (2, 20)
das Messer -
   messerscharf (10, 34)
packen (3, 8)
unterscheiden [1a] (39)

COMMENTS ON GRAMMAR

Extended participle or adjective constructions:

A rather complex construction that occurs frequently, especially in scientific writings, has the formula:

/ modifying word / phrase which modifies a following participle or adjective /
       1   *2*

                / a participle or adjective / a noun /
                         3   *4*

Example:

     / die / zum Zerreißen der Beute / dienenden / Zähne der Katze
        1   2   3   4

This construction is a formal, condensed alternative to a relative clause. The relative-clause formulation of the above example is:

     / die / Zähne der Katze /, die / zum Zerreißen der Beute / dienen
        1   4   2   3

There are several correspondences between extended participle or adjective constructions and their related relative clauses.

    1) A <u>present participle</u> in an extended adjective construction corresponds to an <u>inflected verb</u> in the relative clause. Example:

/ der / in der Lücke zwischen dem Schneidezahn und dem Backenzahn / <u>stehende</u> / Eckzahn

/ der / Eckzahn /, der / in der Lücke zwischen dem Schneidezahn und dem Backenzahn / <u>steht</u>

    2) A <u>past participle</u> in an extended adjective construction corresponds to a <u>passive</u> construction if a <u>process</u> is being described. Examples:

/ das / bei der Papierfabrikation in großen Mengen / <u>gebrauchte</u> / Material

/ das / Material /, das / bei der Papierfabrikation in großen Mengen / <u>gebraucht wird</u>

/ unser / in die Unterwäsche / <u>eingenähtes</u> / Geld

/ unser / Geld /, das / in die Unterwäsche / <u>eingenäht worden ist</u>

    3) A <u>past participle</u> in an extended adjective construction corresponds to the <u>past participle</u> + an <u>inflected form of sein</u> if a <u>condition</u> is being described. Example:

/ das / zum Zerbeißen harter Insekten-Panzer / <u>eingerichtete</u> / Gebiß des Maulwurfs

/ das / Gebiß des Maulwurfs /, das / zum Zerbeißen harter Insekten-Panzer / <u>eingerichtet ist</u>

    4) The <u>descriptive adjective</u> in the extended adjective construction corresponds to the <u>predicate adjective</u> in the relative clause. Example:

/ eine / in der Hitze / <u>zähe</u> / Flüssigkeit

/ eine / Flüssigkeit /, die / in der Hitze / <u>zäh ist</u>

Name _____ Datum _____

Rewrite the following noun + relative clause constructions as extended participle/adjective constructions.

1 die Beute, die von der Katze festgehalten wird,

_____die von der Katze festgehaltene Beute_____

2 die Reißzähne, die bei dem Hund vorhanden sind,

_____

3 die Schneidezähne des Hundes, die in einer Reihe nebeneinander-
  stehen,

_____

_____

4 seine Nahrung, die aus Kleintieren besteht,

_____

5 die Schneidezähne, die hauptsächlich zum Abnagen von Knochen
  dienen,

_____

_____

6 seine Zähne, die mit spitzen Zacken und Höckern versehen sind,

_____

_____

7 die Nahrung, die zwischen den Backenzähnen zerrieben wird,

_____

_____

Rewrite the following extended participle/adjective constructions
as noun + relative clause constructions.

1 diese im Unterkiefer nur noch verkümmert vorhandenen Zähne

_____diese Zähne, die im Unterkiefer nur noch verkümmert vorhanden sind,

2 diese nicht zum Abbeißen von Gräsern taugenden Zähne

_____

_____

3 die Mahlflächen besitzenden Backenzähne

----

4 die zwischen den Schneidezähnen und Backenzähnen stehenden
Eckzähne

----

5 die abgerupfte und zwischen den Mahlzähnen zerriebene Nahrung

----

----

6 die zeitlebens von unten nachwachsenden Nagezähne

----

7 das von Ratten mit diesem Nagen zerstörte Mauerwerk

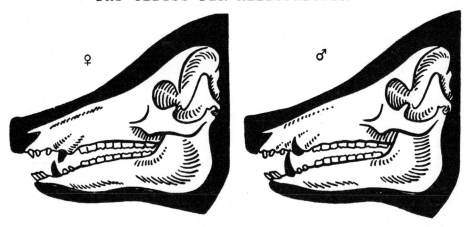

Beim Wildschwein und Hausschwein dienen die Zähne sowohl zum Abbeißen und Zerkleinern der Nahrung als auch zum Kauen. Die starken Eckzähne erleichtern das Aufwühlen des Bodens und das Ausgraben der Nahrung. Die rüsselförmige Schnauze und der keilförmig gebaute Schädel sind Anpassungen an die Ernährungsweise.

Auch der Mensch hat ein Allesfresser-Gebiß. Das Milchgebiß des Kindes besteht nur aus 20 Zähnen, weil jederseits nur die beiden Vorbackenzähne ausgebildet sind.

Durchschnittlich im 6. Lebensjahr beginnt dann der Zahnwechsel. Dabei werden die Milchzähne im Verlaufe mehrerer Jahre nach und nach durch bleibende Zähne ersetzt. Außerdem werden im Ober- und Unterkiefer jederseits 3 Backenzähne neu gebildet. Das voll entwickelte Gebiß besteht aus 32 Zähnen. Viele Menschen haben zeitlebens nur 30 oder 28 Zähne. Der hinterste Backenzahn jeder Kieferhälfte bricht erst sehr spät durch (etwa vom 20. Lebensjahr an) oder bleibt gänzlich unentwickelt. Wegen ihres späten Auftretens nennt man diese Zähne auch Weisheitszähne.

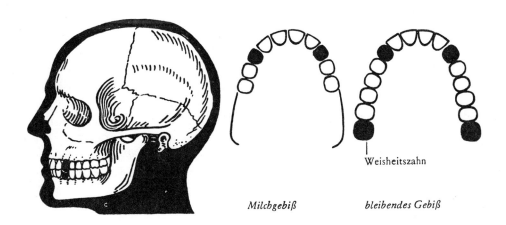

Weisheitszahn

Milchgebiß   *bleibendes Gebiß*

DAS GEBISS DER ALLESFRESSER

Beim Wildschwein und Hausschwein

dienen die Zähne sowohl zum Abbei-
    ßen und Zerkleinern der Nah-
    rung als auch zum Kauen.
Die starken Eckzähne erleichtern
das Aufwühlen des Bodens
5 und das Ausgraben der Nahrung.

Die rüsselförmige Schnauze

und der keilförmig gebaute Schadel

sind Anpassungen an die Ernährungs-
    weise.
Auch der Mensch
10 hat ein Allesfresser-Gebiß.
Das Milchgebiß des Kindes
besteht nur aus 20 Zähnen,
weil jederseits nur die beiden Vor-
    backenzähne ausgebildet sind.
Durchschnittlich im 6. Jahr
15 beginnt dann der Zahnwechsel.
Dabei
werden die Milchzähne
im Verlaufe mehrerer Jahre
nach und nach
20 durch bleibende Zähne ersetzt.
Außerdem
werden im Ober- und Unterkiefer
jederseits
3 Backenzähne
25 neu gebildet.
Das voll entwickelte Gebiß
besteht aus 32 Zähnen.

Viele Menschen haben zeitlebens

nur 30 oder 28 Zähne.
30 Der hinterste Backenzahn
jeder Kieferhälfte
bricht erst sehr spät durch
(etwa vom 20. Lebensjahr an)
oder bleibt gänzlich unentwickelt.
35 Wegen ihres späten Auftretens
nennt man diese Zähne auch Weis-
    heitszähne.

THE TEETH OF OMNIVORES

In the wild boar and the domesti-
    cated pig
the teeth serve for biting off and
    mincing food as well as for
    chewing.
The strong canines facilitate
the grubbing up of the ground
and the digging out of food.
The snout, shaped like the trunk of
    an elephant,
and the cranium, which is constructed
    in the shape of a wedge,
are adaptations to the way of getting
    food.
The human being, too,
has the dentition of an omnivore.
The child's set of milk teeth
consists of only 20 teeth,
because on each side only the two
    front molars are developed.
On the average in the sixth year,
then, begins the changing of teeth.
Hereby (as a result)
the milk teeth,
in the course of several years,
gradually
(are) replaced with permanent teeth.
Moreover,
in the upper and lower jaw,
on each side,
three molars
(are) newly formed.
The fully developed set of teeth
consists of 32 teeth.
Many people have, as long as they
    live,
only 30 or 28 teeth.
The back molar
of each half of the jaw
doesn't break through until very late
(approximately from the 20th year on)
or remains completely undeveloped.
Because of their late appearance,
these teeth are also called wisdom
    teeth.

COMMENTS ON GRAMMAR

Conditional sentences:

A conditional sentence consists of two clauses: an if-clause ("condition") and a then-clause ("conclusion"). The if-clause is a subordinate clause, introduced by **wenn** as the subordinating conjunction. Example:

> Wenn ein Fleischfresser sehr hungrig ist, frißt er manchmal auch Beeren.

Usually the subordinate if-clause precedes the then-clause. In that case, the if-clause is the first element of the sentence and is followed by the inflected verb of the main clause, as in the example above.

Sometimes the comma of the **wenn**-clause is followed by the adverb **so** or **dann**. Examples:

> Wenn ein Fleischfresser sehr hungrig ist, so frißt er manchmal auch Beeren.
> Wenn ein Nagezahn abbricht, dann wächst der gegenüberstehende weiter.

Sometimes **wenn** is omitted. In that case, the inflected verb begins the conditional clause. Example:

> Bricht ein Nagezahn ab, so wächst der gegenüberstehende weiter.

There are three types of conditional sentences:
1) "real conditions"
2) "unreal conditions"
3) "contrary-to-fact conditions"

"Real conditions" have regular present or past tense verb forms. The examples above are all real conditions.

"Unreal" and "contrary-to-fact" conditional sentences have subjunctive forms. [§7.7] The nine auxiliary verbs are especially common in subjunctive forms:

sein: wär-	haben: hätt-	werden: würd-
dürfen: dürft-	können: könnt-	mögen: möcht-
müssen: müßt-	sollen: sollt-	wollen: wollt-

Example of an "unreal" conditional sentence:

> Wenn das Pferd messerscharfe Zähne hätte, so könnte es Hasen und Kühe zerreißen.

Note that when there is no modal in the main clause, usually the auxiliary form **würd-** + infinitive of the main verb is used. Example:

> Wenn ich im Ausland wäre, würde ich meinen Paß immer in der Tasche tragen.

Example of a "contrary-to-fact" conditional sentence:

> Wären die Weisheitszähne unserem zweijährigen Töchterchen durchgebrochen, so hätten wir es schnell zum Zahnarzt gebracht.

Conditional sentences are treated in more detail in §11.

Name _____ Datum _____

Join each pair of sentences into a conditional sentence, start-
ing with the **wenn**-clause.

<u>Real conditions</u>:

1 Ein Kind ist sechs Jahre alt. Gewöhnlich beginnt der Zahnwechsel.

----

2 Die Weisheitszähne bleiben gänzlich unentwickelt. Der Mensch
  hat nur 28 Zähne.

<u>Unreal conditions</u>:

1 Der Hund hat keine Backenzähne. Er kann nicht richtig kauen.

----

2 Pflanzenfresser können schneller laufen als Fleischfresser.
  Diese müssen verhungern (starve).

----

3 In einem Gebiet leben mehr Fleisch- als Pflanzenfresser. Die
  Fleischfresser finden nicht genügend Nahrung.

<u>Review</u>:

Underline the adjective-modifying adverbs in the following:

1 die starken Eckzähne   4 durch bleibende Zähne
2 die rüsselförmige Schnauze   5 das voll entwickelte Gebiß
3 der keilförmig gebaute Schädel 6 bleibt gänzlich unentwickelt

Identify the genitive in each of the following noun + genitive
phrases by checking in the appropriate column.

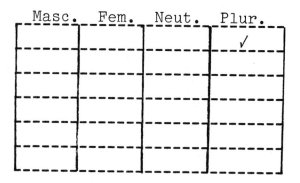

	Masc.	Fem.	Neut.	Plur.
1 das Gebiß der Allesfresser				✓
2 zum Zerkleinern der Nahrung				
3 das Aufwühlen des Bodens				
4 das Milchgebiß des Kindes				
5 im Verlaufe mehrerer Jahre				
6 der hinterste Backenzahn jeder Kieferhälfte				

LITERATUR

FONDUE ODER DER FREITISCH

Der Tisch stand
auf einem rotbraunen Perserteppich,
barocke Nußbaumfüße

von einer Batistdecke überhangen,

in der noch die Schrankfalten zu
      sehen waren.
Vier tiefe und vier flache Teller,
von Löffeln und Gabeln umlegt,
geschliffene Gläser in Tulpenform.
Marga sah das Sofa voller Kissen,

die Standuhr mit hin- und herschwin-
      gendem Sonnenperpendikel,

den schrägen, blendenden Lichtbalken,
der durch die offene Schiebetür eines
      helleren Zimmers fiel.
      Herr Sutor drehte sich
im tiefen Ledersessel
und sah sie stehen.
Er stand auf,
ging die wenigen Schritte zu ihr hin,
gab ihr die Hand,
und sie knickste dabei.
      „Sie sind sicher die Studentin,
die heute unser Gast ist?"
sagte Herr Sutor.
      „Ja."
      „Das ist schön.
Hoffentlich gibt es auch
was Gutes. —
Aber, wo steckt denn meine Frau?"
„Sie hat mich in das Zimmer gebracht
und hier —"
      „Charlotte!" rief Herr Sutor.
— „Kommen Sie," sagte er zu Marga,
„setzen Sie sich ein wenig zu mir."
Er berührte sie am Ellbogen,
rückte den Sessel
und blieb hinter ihr stehen,
bis sie sich gesetzt hatte.
      „Aber, warum nehmt ihr da drüben
            Platz?"
rief Frau Sutor, als sie eintrat.
      „Wenn du dich um unseren Gast
            nicht kümmerst,
ihn einfach ins Zimmer stellst
und verschwindest —"
      „Verschwindest — ich habe zu tun.
Berta ist noch nicht so perfekt,
daß ich sie allein lassen kann.
Und schließlich gibt es Fondue."
      „Fondue?
Gut, dann verzeihe ich alles.

FONDUE, OR THE FREE MEAL

The table stood
on a reddish-brown Persian rug,
baroque walnut legs
covered with a fine linen table
      cover
in which the folds from lying in the
      closet could still be seen.
Four deep and four shallow plates,
laid with spoons and forks,
cut-glass, tulip-shaped goblets.
Marga saw the sofa full of cushions,
the grandfather clock with its
      swinging pendulum which ended
      in a shiny brass disk,
the slanting, dazzling shaft of light
which fell through the open sliding
      door of a brighter room.
      Mr. Sutor turned
in the deep leather armchair
and saw her standing.
He got up,
walked the few steps over to her,
and offered her his hand,
at which she curtsied.
      "You are no doubt the student
who is our guest today?"
said Mr. Sutor.
      "Yes."
      "That's fine.
I hope there'll be
something good. —
But where in the world is my wife?"
"She brought me into the room
and (left me) here —"
      "Charlotte!" called Mr. Sutor.
— "Come," he said to Marga,
"sit down with me a while."
He touched her on the elbow,
moved the armchair,
and remained standing behind her
until she had seated herself.
      "But why are you sitting over
            there?"
cried Mrs. Sutor when she came in.
      "If you don't trouble yourself
            about our guest,
(if you) just stick her in the room
and disappear —"
      "Disappear — I'm busy.
Bertha still isn't perfect enough
that I can leave her alone.
And after all, we're having fondue."
      "Fondue?
Good, then I'll forgive everything.

Fondue oder Der Freitisch

Der Tisch stand auf einem rotbraunen Perserteppich, barocke Nußbaumfüße von einer weißen Batistdecke überhangen,
in der noch die Schrankfalten zu sehen waren. Vier tiefe und
vier flache Teller, von Löffeln und Gabeln umlegt, geschlif-
5 fene Gläser in Tulpenform. Marga sah das Sofa voller Kissen,
die Standuhr mit hin- und herschwingendem Sonnenperpendikel,
den schrägen, blendenden Lichtbalken, der durch die offene
Schiebetür eines helleren Zimmers fiel.
Herr Sutor drehte sich im tiefen Ledersessel und sah sie
10 stehen. Er stand auf, ging die wenigen Schritte zu ihr hin,
gab ihr die Hand, und sie knickste dabei.
„Sie sind sicher die Studentin, die heute unser Gast ist?"
sagte Herr Sutor.
„Ja."
15 „Das ist schön. Hoffentlich gibt es auch was Gutes. —
Aber, wo steckt denn meine Frau?"
„Sie hat mich in das Zimmer gebracht und hier — "
„Charlotte!" rief Herr Sutor. „Charlotte! — Kommen Sie",
sagte er zu Marga, „setzen Sie sich ein wenig zu mir." Er
20 berührte sie am Ellbogen, rückte den Sessel und blieb hinter
ihr stehen, bis sie sich gesetzt hatte.
„Aber, warum nehmt ihr da drüben Platz?" rief Frau Sutor,
als sie eintrat.
„Wenn du dich um unseren Gast nicht kümmerst, ihn einfach
25 ins Zimmer stellst und verschwindest — "
„Verschwindest — ich habe zu tun. Berta ist noch nicht
so perfekt, daß ich sie allein lassen kann. Und schließlich
gibt es Fondue."
„Fondue? Gut, dann verzeihe ich alles. Fondue, das ist
30 großartig! — Mögen Sie auch Fondue?" sagte er und beugte
sich zu Marga hinab.
„Wo bleibt nur Oskar?" Frau Sutor ging aus dem Zimmer. Im
Flur draußen klatschte sie in die Hände und rief: „Oskar!
Oskar!"
35 „Mögen Sie auch Fondue?" fragte Herr Sutor wieder.
„Ich kenne es nicht."
Oskar hatte kleine Augen, Bürstenhaar, er trug ein weißes
Hemd, eine schwarze Hose, die Hände in den Taschen. Frau
Sutor sagte: „Das ist Fräulein — wie war doch der Name?"
40 „Leibold."
„ — Fräulein Leibold, die wir diesmal zum Freitisch
haben."

---

11 sie knickste dabei: *Well-brought-*
up German girls, even in their late
teens and early twenties, often
drop a slight curtsy as a sign of
respect when they meet an older
person for the first time.

15 was = etwas

17 ...und hier (stehengelassen): *But*
it would be impolite to say it.

22 nehmt ihr: *Mrs. Sutor uses the*
familiar plural form ihr *when she*

addresses her husband and the girl,
although the latter is a stranger.

30 großartig - *great*

30 sich hinab·beugen - *incline*

32 Wo bleibt nur...= Wo steckt denn
(16)

33 der Flur - *hall*

37 das Bürstenhaar - *crew cut*

41 der Freitisch - *free meal, to which*
a rich family invites a student

Oskar zog die rechte Hand aus der Tasche und ging zu
Marga hin, die gerade aufstand.

45   Er sah, sie war nicht sein Typ. Der Kopf war etwas zu
groß, und die Nase — die Mädchen im Club trugen flottere
Sachen.

„Warum ziehst du keinen Rock zum Essen an?" fragte Herr
Sutor. „Habe ich es nicht schon tausendmal gesagt, daß ich
50   es wenigstens am Sonntag haben will!"

„Ich fühle mich wohler so, Papa. Und das Essen schmeckt
mir deshalb genauso gut — zudem gibt es Fondue."

„Reden Sie auch so mit Ihrem Papa, Fräulein — wie war der
Name?"

55   „Leibold."

„Fräulein Leibold."

Marga wollte sagen, wie das mit ihrem Vater damals war,
doch Herr Sutor fiel rasch in ihre Gedanken: „Bestimmt nicht!
Wenn ich meinem Vater eine solche Antwort gegeben hätte, wäre
60   ich rausgeflogen und hätte bis Montag in meinem Zimmer ge-
fastet."

„Davon sieht man dir heute nichts mehr an, Papa!"

Frau Sutor klatschte in die Hände, was Herrn Sutor fast
erschreckte; er zog die Hand, die Oskar ohrfeigen wollte, zu-
65   rück.

„Dein Glück," sagte er. Oskar grinste. Herr Sutor schmun-
zelte.

Sie setzten sich, das Mädchen kam ins Zimmer und stellte
die Suppenschüssel in die Tischmitte. Frau Sutor schöpfte
70   aus, eine dicke Tomatensuppe mit Schnittlauch und gebräunten
Zwiebelringen.

„Warum ist es nur so dunkel bei uns?" sagte Herr Sutor.

„Ich mag das so", sagte Frau Sutor.

„Aber ich nicht! Berta, zieh bitte die Vorhänge auf!"

75   Das Mädchen schob die Gardinen zur Seite. Stores hingen
vor den Scheiben. Das Licht des Himmels über leeren Baum-
kronen erhellte das Zimmer.

„Jetzt sehe ich doch wenigstens die Suppe im Teller",
sagte Herr Sutor.

44 gerade - *just (in the act of)*

46 flott - *chic*

48 der Rock = die Jacke

52 deshalb - *that way*

52 zudem = außerdem

53 reden = sprechen

58 doch = aber

58 in ihre Gedanken fallen [7a] -
interrupt her thoughts

58 rasch = schnell

59 Wenn... [§11.3]

59 wäre ich rausgeflogen - *I would
have been thrown out (Literally:
I would have flown out)* — rausgeflogen = <u>her</u>ausgeflogen

60 fasten - *fast*

62 *What can be assumed about Mr. Sutor's appearance?*

63 was: *Indefinite relative pronoun
which refers to the entire preceding clause.*

63 fast = beinah

64 ohrfeigen - *slap*

66 grinsen - *grin wickedly (The verb
grinsen rarely has a pleasant con-
notation.)*

66 schmunzeln - *smirk*

69 die Suppenschüssel - *soup tureen*

69 aus·schöpfen - *ladle out*

70 der Schnittlauch - *chives*

71 die Zwiebel - *onion*

72 nur (32)

74 auf·ziehen [2a] - *open*

74 der Vorhang - *drapery*

75 schieben [2a] - *shove*

75 die Gardine = der Vorhang

75 der Store - *sheer panel curtain*

76 die Scheibe - *window pane*

76 die Baumkrone - *treetop*

77 erhellen - *brighten*

80   „Ich esse nicht viel, sonst schaffe ich die Fondue nicht",
sagte Oskar.

   „Guten Appetit", sagte Frau Sutor, lächelte kurz und gekünstelt zu Marga hinüber, die den Löffel in die Suppe tauchte.

   Alle schwiegen, bis Frau Sutor nach Berta rief. Schon beim
85 ersten Ruf stand Berta auf der Schwelle.

   „Räumen Sie die Teller fort und bringen Sie die Fondue!"
Sie hielt ihren Teller, der noch halb gefüllt war, Berta ent-
gegen.

   Auch Marga hatte noch Suppe im Teller; alle sahen zu ihr
90 herüber, sie hörte auf zu essen, und das Mädchen nahm den
Teller weg.

   Die Fondue wurde in einer Tonpfanne serviert, auf einem
silbernen Öfchen mit blauen Spiritusflammen. Frau Sutor überschüttete die flachen Teller mit Brotwürfeln, die — wie sie
95 erklärte — mit der Gabel aufgespießt, in die Fondue getunkt,
gedreht und rasch zum Mund geführt werden mußten.

   „Sie kennen nicht Fondue?" fragte Herr Sutor.

   „Nein, ich kenne es nicht."

   „Es ist eine Schweizer Spezialität. Meine Frau hat sie
100 aus Zürich mitgebracht.

   „Die hast du ganz prima hingekriegt, Mama!"

   „Schmeckt es Ihnen, Fräulein — ?"

   Marga hatte den ersten Würfel im Mund. Die Fondue war
heiß, klebrig, der Geruch heißen Weins durchsäuerte den Käse,
105 Fäden spannten sich vom Topf zur Gabel.

   „Franzosen und Amerikaner fliegen am Sonntagmittag in die
Schweiz, um Fondue zu essen", sagte Herr Sutor. „Das haben
wir nicht nötig. Wir haben die Fondue auf dem Tisch. Schmeckt
sie nicht großartig?"

110   „Danke, ja."

   „Aber Sie müssen sich dranhalten! So etwas bekommen Sie

80 sonst - *otherwise*
80 schaffen *(wk.) - cope with*
82 gekünstelt - *affectedly*
83 tauchen - *dip*
84 schweigen [1a] = nicht sprechen
84 rufen [7f] (nach) - *call (for)*
85 die Schwelle - *threshold:* auf der Schwelle - *in the doorway*
86 fort·räumen - *clear away*
86 die Fondue: *A loan-word from French, and in most dictionaries it is listed as neuter.*
87 entgegen·halten [7a] *(+ dat.) - hold out (to)*
92 die Tonpfanne - *clay pot*
93 das Öfchen - *little burner*
93 überschütten - *shower, cover*
94 der Würfel - *cube*
94 *The independent sentence which could be made from the relative clause:* Die Brotwürfel mußten mit der Gabel aufgespießt, in die Fon-due getunkt, gedreht und rasch zum

Mund geführt werden. *Notice that the four past participles are all dependent on the auxiliary verb* werden. [§10.3]
95 die Gabel - *fork*
95 auf·spießen - *spear*
95 tunken - *dip*
96 drehen - *turn*
96 rasch (58)
96 geführt = gebracht
101 prima - *first-class*
101 hin·kriegen - *make, prepare*
104 klebrig - *sticky*
104 der Geruch - *odor*
104 heißen Weins [§1.4.1 + §4.7]
104 durchsäuern - *permeate with an acid taste*
104 der Käse - *cheese*
105 sich spannen - *stretch*
105 der Topf = die Pfanne (92)
107 nötig haben - *need*
111 sich dran·halten [7a] - *keep at it*

nicht alle Tage. Mit jedem Bissen wird die Fondue besser.
Das Beste kommt ganz zuletzt. Sehen Sie, der Oskar weiß das,
der kratzt bereits das Dicke vom Topfboden!"
115   „Prima, Mama, hast du sie hingekriegt!"
    „Ich bekomme sie immer hin. Ich nehme die besten Zutaten.
Schmeckt es Ihnen nicht?"
    „Danke, es ist etwas sehr Feines."
    „Ranhalten, immer ranhalten!" sagte Herr Sutor.
120 Das Mädchen goß Wein in die Gläser und ging hinaus.
    „Und was ißt Berta?" fragte Herr Sutor.
    „Berta? — Die Suppe, und Eier soll sie sich backen, meinet-
wegen mit Schinken.
    „Prima, ganz prima, Mama!"
125   „Sie hören ja schon auf! Und haben noch so viele Würfel
im Teller!" sagte Herr Sutor.
    „Ich bin keine große Esserin, die Portionen in der Mensa
sind klein —"
    „Ja, Fondue sättigt", sagte Frau Sutor. „Es sind die
130 besten Käsesorten, teuerster Genever."
    „Prost! Allerseits Prost!" Herr Sutor hob sein Glas und
sah Marga an, die froh war, trinken zu können. Der kühle
Wein tat gut und nahm ihr die Übelkeit für Sekunden.
    Oskar hatte die Pfanne auf seinen Teller gesetzt und drehte
135 darin die letzten Brotwürfel.
    „Prima, ganz prima!"
    „Wenn er in allem so tüchtig wäre wie im Essen —", sagte
Herr Sutor. „Aber hat es auch Ihnen geschmeckt?"
    „Danke, es war ausgezeichnet. — Darf ich mich jetzt ver-
140 abschieden?"
    Wäre die Übelkeit nicht gewesen, sie hätte nicht den Mut
gefunden, so unvermittelt aufzustehen.
    Marga reichte Frau Sutor, Herrn Sutor, der sich dabei er-
hob und die Serviette zerknüllte, zuletzt Oskar die Hand.
145   „Das ist nicht nett, daß Sie uns so schnell verlassen",
sagte Herr Sutor.

112 der Bissen - *bite*
113 zuletzt = am Ende
114 kratzen - *scratch*
114 bereits = schon
114 das Dicke - *goop*
116 Ich bekomme sie immer hin. - *It*
always turns out right for me.
116 die Zutaten *(pl.)* - *ingredients*
118 etwas ... Feines [§5.5.2]
119 ranhalten = sich dranhalten (111)
120 gießen [2a] - *pour*
122 sich ein Ei backen - *fry an egg*
for oneself
122 meinetwegen - *for all I care*
123 der Schinken - *ham*
127 die Mensa - *student cafeteria*
129 sättigen - *satisfy*
130 teuer = <u>nicht</u> billig

130 der Genever - *gin*
131 allerseits - *to everybody, all*
around
131 heben [2d] - *raise*
133 gut tun [§6.2.2] - *be refreshing*
133 nehmen [5c] - *(here) take away*
133 die Übelkeit - *nausea*
137 tüchtig - *diligent*
139 ausgezeichnet - *excellent*
139 sich verabschieden - *say good-bye*
141 der Mut - *courage*
142 unvermittelt - *abruptly*
143 Marga reichte ... die Hand - *shook*
hands with ...
143 sich erheben [2d] = auf·stehen
144 die Serviette - *napkin*
144 zerknüllen - *crush*
145 nett - *nice*

„Es war schön bei Ihnen", sagte Marga, und es fiel ihr
nicht schwer, glücklich zu lächeln.
        Draußen im Flur half ihr Herr Sutor in den Mantel. Die
150 Handschuhe fielen zu Boden, sie bückte sich danach, und dabei
hörte sie Oskar im Zimmer sagen: „Hoffentlich kommt nächsten
Sonntag nicht wieder so 'ne Ziege!"
        „Psst", zischte die Mama.
        „Beehren Sie uns wieder einmal", sagte Herr Sutor.
155   Sie selber öffnete die Tür.
        „Einen schönen Sonntag wünsch' ich!" rief er nach.
        Auf dem Gartenweg hielt sie die Hand vor den Mund und
atmete tief die februarkalte Luft.

— Hans Bender (1919-   )

149 der Flur (33)
150 der Handschuh - *glove*
150 sich bücken - *stoop*
152 die Ziege = (hier) dummes Mädchen
    - *goat*

154 beehren - *honor*
156 nach•rufen [7f] - *call out*
158 atmen - *breathe, inhale*

Du bist wie eine Blume

Du bist wie eine Blume
so hold und schön und rein;
ich schau' dich an, und Wehmut
schleicht mir ins Herz hinein.

Mir ist, als ob ich die Hände
aufs Haupt dir legen sollt',
betend, daß Gott dich erhalte
so rein und schön und hold.

— Heinrich Heine
(1797-1856)

*This poem has been set to music
by several composers; one of the
best-known versions is that of
Robert Schumann.*

2 hold - *wholesome and appealing*
3 die Wehmut - *sadness, melancholy*

4 schleichen [1b] = ganz leise gehen
5 mir ist - *it seems to me*
6 aufs Haupt = auf den Kopf
6 dir [§1.3.5]
7 beten - *pray* [§9.2.8]
7 erhalten [7a] - *keep*

QUESTIONS ON THE TEXT

Fondue oder Der Freitisch

*What does the author accomplish with
    his description of the room?*
Who is Marga?
Why is she in this house?
Who let her in?
*Why is Mr. Sutor annoyed with Mrs.
    Sutor?*
What is her excuse?
Who is Berta?
Who is Oskar?
How is he dressed?
*What does Mrs. Sutor have to do in
    order to introduce Marga to
    Oskar?*
What does Oskar think of Marga?
To whom does he compare her?
*How does Oskar indicate his feelings
    of social responsibility — or
    lack of them — toward Marga?*
*How does he express courtesy — or
    lack of it — toward her?*
*What is Oskar's attitude toward his
    father?*
*Is there a corresponding feeling from
    father to son? (Give examples.)*
What is the first course?
When is it cleared from the table?
Why at that time?
*Who, if anyone, finishes the first
    course?*
What is the main course?
How is it eaten?
Why is Mrs. Sutor's always so good?
How does it taste to Marga?
*To whom does it taste particularly
    good?*
*Why, in Mr. Sutor's opinion, should
    Marga eat more?*
*What excuse does she give for not
    eating more?*
*Why is Mrs. Sutor's fondue always
    so good?*
What will Berta eat?
*How does Marga finally get away from
    the table?*
How does she feel?
Who takes her to the door?
Who helps her into her coat?
Who picks up her glove?
Who opens the door for her?
What remark does she hear behind her?
What revives her?

*Give several examples of the family's
    courtesy — or lack of it —
    toward Marga and each other.*

Wer ist Marga?
Bei was für einer Familie soll Marga
    an diesem Sonntag essen?
Wie kommt es, daß die Familie Marga
    eingeladen hat?
Wie heißen die Mitglieder der Fami-
    lie?
Wer ist Berta?
Wie benimmt sich die Familie vor dem
    Gast?
Was sagt Herr Sutor, zum Beispiel,
    zu seiner Frau?
Was sagt er zu seinem Sohn?
Geben Sie noch einige Beispiele von
    der Höflichkeit — oder Unhöf-
    lickeit — der Familie!
Was ist das erste Gericht bei Tisch?
    (Ein Gericht ist eine Speise:
    was man ißt.)
Wieviel darf Marga davon essen?
Warum wird es weggenommen?
Was ist das Hauptgericht?
Wie ißt man es?
Wie schmeckt es Marga?
Wie schmeckt es Oskar? (Woher wissen
    wir das?)
Was tut Marga am Ende?
Wer bringt sie zur Tür?
Beschreiben Sie die Szene vor der
    Tür!
Was hört sie hinter sich?
Kann man sagen, daß Marga ein will-
    kommener Gast war?

Du bist wie eine Blume

Who is talking to whom?
Why is the poet sad?
*What is the poet trying to prevent
    with his prayer?*

WORDS AND WORD FAMILIES

auf·hören (90, 125)
auf·stehen (10, 44, 142)
drehen (96, 134)
    sich drehen (9)
flach (4, 94)
die Gabel -n (4, 95)
großartig (30, 109)
heben [2d] (131)
    sich erheben (143)
hell (8)
    erhellen (77)
das Hemd -en (38)
der Löffel - (4, 83)
-mal:
    diesmal (41)
    einmal (154)
    tausendmal (49)
mögen [§6.1.3] (30, 35, 73)

die Pfanne -n (134)
    die Tonpfanne -n (92)
prima (101, 115, 124)
rasch (58, 96)
rufen [7f] (33, 84)
    nach·rufen (156)
    der Ruf -e (85)
schieben [2a] (75)
    die Schiebetür (8)
der Sessel - (20)
    der Ledersessel (9)
verschwinden [3a] (25, 26)
der Würfel - (103, 125)
    der Brotwürfel (94)
ziehen [2a] (43)
    an·ziehen (48)
    auf·ziehen (74)
    zurück·ziehen (64)

Name _____ Datum _____

Review the rules for pronunciation of compound and prefixed verbs, pages 53-54. Then underline the stressed syllable in each of the following verb forms. The number with each form indicates its location in the text.

1 über<u>han</u>gen (2)

2 umlegt (4)

3 berührte (20)

4 eintrat (23)

5 verzeihe (29)

6 aufstand (44)

7 rausgeflogen (60)

8 erhellte (77)

9 überschüttete (93)

10 mitgebracht (100)

11 hingekriegt (101)

12 durchsäuerte (104)

13 dranhalten (111)

14 verabschieden (139)

15 aufzustehen (142)

16 zerknüllte (144)

Look up the line reference given in the left margin and answer the question on that passage.

24 Why is **ihn** translated "her"?

----

44 die gerade aufstand: Rewrite this relative clause as an independent sentence, using the antecedent of the relative pronoun in your new sentence.

----

90 sie hörte auf zu essen: Which translation is suitable? — She stopped eating. She stopped to eat.

----

143 der sich...: Rewrite the relative clause as an independent sentence, using the antecedent of the relative pronoun in your new sentence.

Review the Notes on Language, pages 21 and 52, regarding the use of the definite article instead of the possessive adjective with

parts of the body and clothing. Find three examples of this
usage in the poem, **Du bist wie eine Blume**. Copy out the phrases
in which they occur.

1 _____

2 _____

3 _____

COMMENTS ON GRAMMAR

<u>Direct and indirect discourse</u>:

The exact words of a remark constitute the "direct discourse" form. Example:

> *She says, "I'm coming right away."*

The "indirect discourse" form is expressed with certain grammatical adaptations:

> *She says she is coming right away.*
> *She says that she is coming right away.*

German is similar. Direct discourse:

> Sie sagt: „Ich komme gleich."

Indirect discourse:

> Sie sagt, sie kommt gleich.
> Sie sagt, daß sie gleich kommt.

Note the differences in punctuation and the fact that **daß** makes a dependent clause out of the quotation.

When a German reports informally in the present tense something someone does or says, he normally uses indicative verb forms. Read §12.1 of the Grammar Reference Notes (including all subsections) and study the various patterns of grammatical adaptation between direct and indirect discourse. Note also that in direct discourse, the preposition **zu** is used with **sagen**; it is not used in indirect discourse.

> Frau Sutor sagt <u>zu</u> Herrn Sutor: „Ich habe zu tun."
> Frau Sutor sagt Herrn Sutor, daß sie zu tun hat.

Turn now to page 115 and write Exercise A. This will give you practice with the changes in personal pronouns and word order between direct and indirect discourse, using ordinary indicative verb forms. When you have finished the ten sentences of Exercise A, study the "quotative" forms on page 114 and then write Exercise B on page 116.

"Quotative" forms in indirect discourse:

In a formal report — like a newspaper account or a radio or TV news report — the indirect quotation regularly has the inflected verb in a special quotative form. The use of such special quotative forms emphasizes the fact that the person reporting the remark or conversation takes no responsibility for its accuracy.

In indirect discourse the "quoter" is almost always reporting what one other speaker has said. The quotative form thus almost always occurs in the third-person singular. The special quotative form of the third-person singular is the infinitive stem (infinitive - -en/-n) + -e. Examples:

> er/sie trage, liebe, tue, halte, gebe, könne, solle

There is also a special quotative form used in the first-person singular of the modal auxiliaries and **wissen**: the infinitive stem + -e. Examples:

> ich dürfe, könne, möge, müsse, solle, wolle, wisse

The verb **sein** has special forms for the entire conjugation:

ich sei	wir seien
du seiest	ihr seiet
er/sie/es sei	sie seien

The above forms are called subjunctive I and are discussed more fully in §7.6 of the Grammar Reference Notes.

Subjunctive I forms are correct usage for indirect discourse in the third-person singular of all verbs, in the first-person singular of the modal auxiliaries and **wissen**, and in the verb **sein**. However, subjunctive II forms [§7.7] are used for all other persons, and they are often found even in situations where subjunctive I forms are correct usage.

Examples of direct and indirect discourse in a formal report. Notice the correspondence of tenses and verb phrases.

Direct discourse	Indirect discourse
Frau Sutor sagte: „Ich <u>habe</u> viel zu tun."	Frau Sutor sagte, daß sie viel zu tun <u>habe/hätte</u>.
Frau Sutor sagte: „Ich <u>hatte</u> viel zu tun."	Frau Sutor sagte, daß sie viel zu tun <u>gehabt habe/gehabt hätte</u>.
Frau Sutor sagte: „Ich <u>werde</u> viel zu tun <u>haben</u>."	Frau Sutor sagte, daß sie viel zu tun <u>haben werde/haben würde</u>.
Ich berichtete: „Ich <u>habe</u> zu viel zu tun."	Ich berichtete, daß ich zu viel zu tun <u>hätte</u>.
Ich sagte: „Das <u>kann</u> ich nicht versprechen."	Ich sagte, daß ich das nicht versprechen <u>könne/könnte</u>.

A good rule of thumb is that the more formal the report, the more likely it is that subjunctive I forms will be used. They occur frequently in literary prose.

Look at additional examples in §12.3-5. Then write out Exercise B on page 116.

Exercise A:

Rewrite the following direct discourse as indirect discourse,
using indicative forms of the verb but making changes in pronouns,
word order, etc.

1 Frau Sutor sagt: "Ich habe zu tun."

_____ Frau Sutor sagt, sie hat zu tun. / Frau Sutor sagt, daß sie zu tun hat. _____

2 Sie sagt: „Ich kann Berta nicht allein lassen."

----

3 Herr Sutor fragt Marga: „Mögen Sie Fondue?"

----

4 Marga antwortet: „Ich kenne es nicht."

----

5 Herr Sutor fragt seinen Sohn: „Warum ziehst du keinen Rock an?"

----

6 Oskar sagt zu seinem Vater: „Ich fühle mich wohler so."

----

7 Herr Sutor fragt: „Warum ist es so dunkel bei uns?"

----

8 Herr Sutor sagt zu Berta: „Zieh die Vorhänge auf!"

----

9 Frau Sutor sagt zu Berta: „Räumen Sie die Teller fort!"

----

10 Herr Sutor fragt Marga: „Schmeckt die Fondue nicht großartig?"

Exercise B:

After reading the section on quotative forms in the Comments on Grammar, rewrite the following direct discourse as indirect discourse, using subjunctive forms and making changes in pronouns, word order, etc.

1 Herr Sutor fragte Marga: „Reden Sie auch so mit Ihrem Papa?"

_____ Herr Sutor fragte Marga, ob sie auch so mit ihrem Papa rede/redete. _____

2 Oskar sagte zu seinem Vater: „Vom Fasten sieht man dir nichts mehr an!"

----

3 Frau Sutor sagte: „Ich mag es dunkel."

----

4 Marga erzählte ihren Freunden später: „Das Mädchen nahm meinen Teller weg."

----

5 Sie sagte zu ihnen: „Die Fondue hat gar nicht gut geschmeckt."

----

6 Sie fügte hinzu: „Hoffentlich werde ich diese Familie nie wieder sehen."

GRAMMAR REFERENCE NOTES

TABLE OF CONTENTS

§1. *THE CASES*

1.1. <u>Nominative</u> [For endings of noun modifiers see §4.1-7.]
1.1.1. Subject of a clause.
1.1.2. In the predicate after **sein** or **werden**.

1.2. <u>Accusative</u> [For endings of noun modifiers see §4.1-7.]
1.2.1. Direct object of most verbs.
1.2.2. Object of the prepositions **bis, durch, für, gegen, ohne, um, wider**.
1.2.3. Object of the prepositions **an, auf, hinter, in, neben, über, unter, vor, zwischen** when the preposition + object refers to a destination, a goal, or a target of some kind. These prepositions are also used in expressions of time and idiomatically after certain verbs or adjectives. In such expressions, **auf** and **über** are followed by the accusative. Example of time: **übers Wochenende**; examples with adjectives: **erstaunt über, stolz auf, zornig über/auf**; examples with verbs: **achten auf, sich aufregen über, sich freuen auf** (look forward to), **sich freuen über** (be happy about), **hoffen auf, rechnen auf, warten auf**. Other common idioms consisting of verb + preposition + accusative are: **denken an, erinnern an** (remind of), **sich erinnern an** (remember), **glauben an, gehören in** (belong in).
1.2.4. Extent of time or distance: **Den ganzen Abend** muß Karin über ihren Büchern sitzen. Der Hauptbahnhof ist nur **einen Kilometer** vom Hotel entfernt.

1.3. <u>Dative</u> [For endings of noun modifiers see §4.1-7. The dative form of all plural nouns except those with the ending **-s** ends in **-n**.]
1.3.1. Indirect object of a verb. <u>Note</u>: When a verb has two objects, one a person, the other a thing, the noun or pronoun referring to the person is almost always dative.
1.3.2. There are some verbs whose only object is dative. Examples: **antworten, begegnen, danken, dienen, drohen, fehlen, folgen, gefallen, gehören, gelingen, genügen, gratulieren, helfen, nachgeben, nachlaufen, schaden, schmecken, schmeicheln, winken**.
1.3.3. Object of the prepositions **aus, bei, mit, nach, seit, von, zu**.
1.3.4. Object of the prepositions **an, auf, hinter, in, neben, über, unter, vor, zwischen** when followed by an expression of time (exceptions: **auf, über**: §1.2.3), or when the preposition + object does not refer to a destination or goal [§1.2.3]. These prepositions are also used idiomatically with verbs or adjectives. In such idioms, **vor** is followed by the dative: **sich fürchten vor, sich hüten vor, sich schämen vor**. Other idioms consisting of verb + preposition + dative are: **arbeiten an, erkranken an, hängen an, liegen an, sterben an**.
1.3.5. To indicate a person involved in or affected by a situation: Ich bin **ihm** dankbar. Es geht **dem Kanzler** ziemlich

schlecht. Das tut **mir** leid. Der Koffer ist **der alten Dame** viel zu schwer. Ich schrie **ihr** ins Gesicht. Ich habe **mir** den Arm gebrochen. (I broke <u>my</u> arm.) Der Hundefänger kraulte **dem Hund** den Hals. (The dogcatcher scratched <u>the dog's</u> throat.)

1.4. <u>Genitive</u> [For endings of noun modifiers see §4.1-7. All neuter and most masculine nouns have -s or -es endings in the genitive singular. For exceptions, see §2.3 and §2.4.]

1.4.1. A noun which describes or limits another noun in some way is in the genitive case. The genitive is the case that is related to the English possessive with <u>-'s</u> or <u>-s'</u> endings, or the prepositional phrase with <u>of</u>.

1.4.2. An idiomatic "genitive of manner" consists of an adjective + noun: **reinen Gewissens** (with a clear conscience), **festen Schrittes** (with a firm tread). This construction is characteristic of a formal literary style.

1.4.3. There are many prepositions which are used with the genitive in formal German, especially written German. Some of these prepositions are occasionally used in spoken German; when so used, they are followed by genitive forms in formal speech (lectures, sermons, classical drama), by dative forms in informal speech. Some common ones are: **anstatt, statt, trotz, während, wegen.** Prepositions ending in -halb: **außerhalb, innerhalb, oberhalb, unterhalb** are followed by the genitive in formal German. In conversation they are commonly followed by **von +** dative forms.

§2. *GENDERS OF NOUNS*

2.1. There are several hundred basic nouns, mainly of one or two syllables, whose grammatical gender has no obvious logical connection with meaning. These basic nouns and their genders are learned in early childhood by native speakers of German; foreigners using German have to learn the genders by memorizing them or by meeting them so frequently that they are known and used almost as automatically as they are by the native speakers.
Many German nouns have suffixes that mark both the gender and the plural class. Some of the most important of these suffixes are described in sections 2-4 below. [See also §9.1.]

2.2. Some common feminine and neuter suffixes (plural endings are given in parentheses):
2.2.1. die **-heit, -keit** (-en): die Einheit, die Möglichkeit
2.2.2. die **-ung** (-en): die Kleidung, die Übung, die Zeitung
2.2.3. die **-schaft** (-en): die Feindschaft, die Landschaft
2.2.4. die **-ei** (-en): die Polizei, die Spielerei, die Wäscherei
2.2.5. die **-ik** (-en): die Fabrik, die Logik, die Musik, die Physik (But: **der Atlantik, der Pazifik.**)
2.2.6. die **-in** (-nen): die Arbeiterin, die Berlinerin, die Schriftstellerin

2.2.7. die -tät (-en): die Elektrizität, die Universität
2.2.8. die -sion, -tion (-en): die Inflation, die Kommission,
    die Manipulation, die Revision, die Station
2.2.9. das ¨chen (-): das Blättchen, das Mädchen
2.2.10. das ¨lein (-): das Blümlein, das Fräulein
2.2.11. das/die -nis (-nisse): das Bekenntnis, das Ergebnis,
    das Erlebnis, das Gefängnis, das Geheimnis, das Hin-
    dernis, das Verhältnis, das Verständnis; die Bitternis,
    die Erlaubnis, die Finsternis, die Kenntnis. [See also
    §9.1.]

2.3. Most nouns ending in -e are feminine: die Asche, die Auf-
    gabe, die Nase, die Suppe, die Wolke, die Schnauze, die
    Rose, die Gebärde.
    There are exceptions: das Ende, das Auge, and most of those
    with the prefix Ge-: das Gebirge, das Gebäude, das Gemäl-
    de, das Gerippe.
    In addition, there are numerous nouns referring to male
    beings that end in -e: der Junge, der Knabe, der Löwe, der
    Kunde, der Beamte, der Titane, der Däne, der Biologe, der
    Theologe. The masculine nouns ending in -e are all "weak
    nouns," that is, all the case forms except the nominative
    singular end in -n:

	Singular	Plural
Nom.	der Junge	die Jungen
Acc.	den Jungen	die Jungen
Dat.	dem Jungen	den Jungen
Gen.	des Jungen	der Jungen

2.4. Nouns which refer to human beings and have the suffixes
    -ist, -ant/-ent, -graph are also weak. These have case
    forms like Junge above.
2.4.1. der -ist (Acc. den -isten): der Polizist, der Kommunist,
    der Extremist, der Telephonist, der Pessimist.
2.4.2. der -ant/-ent (Acc. den -anten/-enten): der Fabrikant,
    der Spekulant; der Agent, der Präsident, der Student.
    Caution: Some nouns ending in -ent do not refer to hu-
    man beings and do not belong to the weak masculine class.
    Examples: das Talent / die Talente; das Element / die
    Elemente; das Parlament / die Parlamente. Most such
    nouns are neuter.
2.4.3. der -graph (Acc. den -graphen): der Bibliograph, der
    Geograph, der Photograph; also: der Philosoph / den
    Philosophen.
2.4.4. All the above weak masculine nouns have their feminine
    counterparts ending in -in [§2.2.6]: die Polizistin,
    die Bibliographin, die Korrespondentin.

    Note: All the weak masculine nouns in sections 2.4.1.-2.4.3.
    are pronounced with the stress on the suffix: der Pessimist,
    der Photograph. The stress is on the same syllable in the
    feminine nouns of section 2.4.4: die Agentin, die Photo-
    graphin, and the neuter nouns in the note to 2.4.2: das Ta-
    lent, das Parlament.

2.5. Nouns can be formed from infinitives. All these nouns are neuter: das **Lachen**, das **Reisen**. These "infinitive nouns" often correspond to English nouns ending in "-ing:" Laugh-ing is out of place on a solemn occasion. Traveling can be an important educational experience.

2.6. Nouns can be formed from adjectives, present participles, and past participles. These "nominalized" adjectives and participles have the regular adjective endings [§4.5-7]; in print they are capitalized to show that they are functioning as nouns.

2.6.1. Pure adjectives: der **Alte** (the old man), ein **Alter** (an old man); die Alte, eine Alte; das Alte und das Neue; Altes und Neues.

2.6.2. Present participles: der Reisende, ein Reisender; die Liebenden; das Kommende; die Führende.

2.6.3. Past participles: der Angestellte; die Gefragte; das Mit-gebrachte.

Note: A noun formed from a participle or an adjective often does not appear as a noun in a dictionary, nor does it have a one-word counterpart in English. For example: die Gefrag-te (the woman who is/was asked); das Mitgebrachte (what is/was brought along, the thing that is/was brought along).

§3. *NOUN PLURALS*

The plurals of nouns are distinguished from singulars by several different signals. [For dative plural see §1.3.]

3.1. For some nouns there is an ending.

		Singular	Plural
3.1.1.	-n	die Feder	die Federn
		die Sprache	die Sprachen
3.1.2.	-en	die Frau	die Frauen
		die Tür	die Türen
3.1.3.	-nen	die Königin	die Königinnen
3.1.4.	-e	das Jahr	die Jahre
		der Tag	die Tage
3.1.5.	-er	das Ei	die Eier
		das Kleid	die Kleider
3.1.6.	-s	das Baby	die Babys
		das Hotel	die Hotels
		das Radio	die Radios

3.2. For some nouns the main vowel has Umlaut.

	Singular	Plural
¨	der Bruder	die Brüder
	der Hafen	die Häfen
	der Mantel	die Mäntel
	die Tochter	die Töchter

3.3. For some nouns there is a combination of Umlaut and ending.

		Singular	Plural
3.3.1.	⸚e	der Ball	die Bälle
		die Hand	die Hände
		der Kopf	die Köpfe
3.3.2.	⸚er	der Gott	die Götter
		das Land	die Länder

3.4. For some nouns the plural form is the same as the singular; then the reader must pay close attention to the form of any modifier or, in the case of a subject, to the form of the verb. Only a few masculine and neuter nouns are in this class.

Singular	Plural
unser Dampfer	unsere Dampfer
ein Fenster	zwei Fenster (mehrere Fenster)
das Gemälde	die Gemälde
ein dummes Mädchen	dumme Mädchen
sein Wagen	seine Wagen

3.5. A few nouns have highly irregular plurals, for example: der **Stock** (floor, story of a building), die **Stockwerke**; der **Bau** / die **Bauten**. Many nouns ending in **-mann** have the plural **-leute**:

	Singular	Plural
	der Bergmann	die Bergleute
	der Fachmann	die Fachleute
	der Kaufmann	die Kaufleute
However:	der Staatsmann	die Staatsmänner

3.6.1. Neuter or masculine nouns expressing amount keep their singular form when modified by numbers.

	Singular	Plural
	ein Pfund Butter	zwei Pfund Butter
	ein Dollar	zehn Dollar
	ein Dutzend Eier	vier Dutzend Eier
	ein Paar Schuhe	sieben Paar Schuhe
	ein Glas Bier	drei Glas Bier
But:	Zwei Gläser standen auf dem Tisch.	

3.6.2. Feminine nouns expressing amount have plural forms when modified by numbers.

	Singular	Plural
	eine Million	zwei Millionen
	eine Milliarde	drei Milliarden
	eine Tonne	zehn Tonnen
	eine dänische Krone	25 dänische Kronen
Exception:	eine Mark	50 Mark

§4. *NOUN MODIFIERS*

4.1. Case-and-number endings of der:

	Masc.	Fem.	Neut.	Plur.
Nom.	der	die	das	die
Acc.	den	die	das	die
Dat.	dem	der	dem	den
Gen.	des	der	des	der

4.2. Case-and-number endings of dies-, jed-, jen-, manch-, solch-, welch-, all-:

	Masc.	Fem.	Neut.	Plur.
Nom.	-er	-e	-es	-e
Acc.	-en	-e	-es	-e
Dat.	-em	-er	-em	-en
Gen.	-es	-er	-es	-er

4.3. Case endings of ein:

	Masc.	Fem.	Neut.	Plur.*
Nom.	-	-e	-	
Acc.	-en	-e	-	
Dat.	-em	-er	-em	
Gen.	-es	-er	-es	

4.4. Case-and-number endings of kein, mein, dein, sein, ihr, Ihr, unser, euer:

	Masc.	Fem.	Neut.	Plur.
Nom.	-	-e	-	-e
Acc.	-en	-e	-	-e
Dat.	-em	-er	-em	-en
Gen.	-es	-er	-es	-er

4.5. Case-and-number endings of descriptive adjectives after der or dies-words:

	Masc.	Fem.	Neut.	Plur.
Nom.	-e	-e	-e	-en
Acc.	-en	-e	-e	-en
Dat.	-en	-en	-en	-en
Gen.	-en	-en	-en	-en

4.6. Case-and-number endings of descriptive adjectives after ein or kein-words:

	Masc.	Fem.	Neut.	Plur.
Nom.	-er	-e	-es	-en
Acc.	-en	-e	-es	-en
Dat.	-en	-en	-en	-en
Gen.	-en	-en	-en	-en

4.7. Case-and-number endings of adjectives not preceded by either dies- or kein-words:

	Masc.	Fem.	Neut.	Plur.
Nom.	-er	-e	-es	-e
Acc.	-en	-e	-es	-e
Dat.	-em	-er	-em	-en
Gen.	-en	-er	-en	-er

*There is no plural of ein as limiting modifier: ein Land / Länder. The plural forms einige, ein paar, mehrere, viele are used to indicate some plural concepts: ein Land / viele Länder; ein Kind / ein paar Kinder; eine Frau / mehrere Frauen.

4.8. Comparison of adjectives

4.8.1.1. German adjectives have three "degrees of comparison:" positive, comparative, superlative. These are like English "small, smaller, smallest." The degrees of comparison are shown in German by the endings -er and -(e)st. German does not have a usage like English "more complicated, most complicated." The corresponding German is **komplizierter, kompliziertest-.**
Comparative and superlative adjective modifiers of nouns have the regular descriptive adjective endings [§4.5-7] added after the -er and -(e)st endings. Thus: **eine breitere Fläche, der wichtigste Bestandteil.**

4.8.1.2. A "principal parts" listing of adjectives consists of the simple (positive) degree, the comparative, and the superlative. The positive and comparative degrees are given in the endingless form, the superlative in the **am ...sten** formula. Examples:

Positive	Comparative	Superlative
klein	kleiner	am kleinsten
traurig	trauriger	am traurigsten
unbekannt	unbekannter	am unbekanntesten

4.8.1.3. Some adjectives have Umlaut of the stem vowel in their comparative and superlative forms. Examples:

Positive	Comparative	Superlative
groß	größer	am größten
jung	jünger	am jüngsten
kalt	kälter	am kältesten

Some have different consonants or entirely different stems. Examples:

hoch (hoh-)	höher	am höchsten
nah	näher	am nächsten
viel	mehr	am meisten
gern	lieber	am liebsten
gut	besser	am besten

4.8.2. Special usages with the comparative and superlative:
The comparative may have the meaning "rather, somewhat." Examples: **ein älterer Herr, eine längere Zeit.**
The expression "immer + comparative" corresponds to English "more and more..." Examples:
> **immer schmutziger** (dirtier and dirtier)
> **immer besser** (better and better)
> **immer interessanter** (more and more interesting)

Special superlative forms may be used in the meaning of "extremely." Examples:
Ich bin aufs höchste überrascht. (...extremely surprised)
kleinste Teilchen (very tiny particles)

4.9. Adjectives without endings

An adjective that does not precede the noun it modifies has no ending. **Das ist ein großes Haus. / Das Haus ist groß.**
<u>Note</u>: An adjective may itself be modified. These modifiers are called adverbs, and they have no ending. Note the difference in meaning between: **ein angenehm kühler Tag** (a pleasant<u>ly</u> cool day) and **ein angenehmer, kühler Tag.**

§5. *PRONOUNS*

5.1. The personal pronouns ("Personal" refers to first or second or third grammatical "person.")

		Singular	Plural
1st Person	Nom.	ich	wir
	Acc.	mich	uns
	Dat.	mir	uns
	Gen.	meiner	unser
2nd Person (familiar)	Nom.	du	ihr
	Acc.	dich	euch
	Dat.	dir	euch
	Gen.	deiner	euer
2nd Person (formal)	Nom.	Sie	Sie
	Acc.	Sie	Sie
	Dat.	Ihnen	Ihnen
	Gen.	Ihrer	Ihrer

		Masc.	Fem.	Neut.	
3rd Person	Nom.	er	sie	es	sie
	Acc.	ihn	sie	es	sie
	Dat.	ihm	ihr	ihm	ihnen
	Gen.	seiner	ihrer	seiner	ihrer

5.2. The emphatic and the relative pronouns:

Nom.	der	die	das	die
Acc.	den	die	das	die
Dat.	dem	der	dem	denen
Gen.	dessen	deren	dessen	derer (emphatic) deren (relative)

The emphatic and the relative pronouns have the same forms, except for the genitive plural, and they are also similar to the forms of the definite article [§4.1]. See §13.1 for clues to recognition.

5.3. Factors determining the appropriate pronoun form:
The antecedent of a relative, emphatic, or personal pronoun determines its gender (if singular) or number; its case is determined by its use in its own clause.

5.3.1. Personal pronoun: **Ein armer Mann** fand eine Geldbörse, und
Masc. sing.

der Fund verwirrte **ihm** den Kopf.
Dat.

5.3.2. Relative pronoun: **Der arme Mann, dem** der Fund den Kopf
Masc. sing.   Dat.

verwirrt hatte, wanderte in die Stadt.

	Masc.	Fem.	Neut.	Plural
Nom.				
Acc.				
Dat.				Use in
Gen.				clause

Antecedent

The chart illustrates how the selection in both examples

was made. The lines cross at the pronoun **ihm** for the personal pronouns [§5.1. 3rd person] and at **dem** for the relatives [§5.2].

5.4. Reflexive and reciprocal pronouns

5.4.1. An accusative or dative pronoun which refers to the same
person or thing as the subject is a reflexive pronoun.
The reflexive pronouns of the 1st and 2nd persons are the
same as the regular accusative and dative personal pronouns:

[ich] mich, mir	[wir] uns
[du] dich, dir	[ihr] euch

Examples: Ich ziehe **mich** an. Ich muß **mir** einen neuen
Mantel kaufen. Du lobst **dich** immer. Wir möchten **uns**
hier hinsetzen. Ihr sprecht wenig von **euch**. Ich habe
kein Geld bei **mir**.
In the 3rd person, the reflexive pronoun is **sich**. It is
used as either accusative or dative object, in connection
with subjects in all three genders, either singular or
plural, and with the 2nd person formal subject **Sie**.
Examples: Großpapa zieht **sich** an. Erich lobt **sich** immer.
Sie muß **sich** einen neuen Mantel kaufen. Die Kinder möchten **sich** hier hinsetzen. Warum sprechen Sie so wenig von
sich? Er hat kein Geld bei **sich**.

5.4.2. The plural pronouns **uns**, **euch**, **sich** are used as reciprocal pronouns, meaning "each other." Sie küßten **sich**.
Ich habe es längst gewußt: ihr liebt **euch**.
Note: If there is a likelihood of misunderstanding a
reciprocal pronoun, the word **einander** is used: Wir sehen
einander nur selten. Sie rauften **einander** die Haare aus.

5.5. Indefinite pronouns

5.5.1. The indefinite pronouns **man**, **jemand**, **niemand**, **wer** are
used when human beings are involved; they do not have
distinctive masculine and feminine forms.
The case forms of these pronouns:

Nom.	man	jemand	niemand	wer
Acc.	einen	jemanden	niemanden	wen
Dat.	einem	jemandem	niemandem	wem
Gen.	sein	jemandes	niemandes	wessen

Often **einer** and **keiner** are used as indefinite pronouns
without specific reference to male or female beings.

5.5.2. The inanimate (neuter) pronouns are **etwas** and **nichts**.
They do not have distinctive accusative and dative forms.
These pronouns are often used in combination with adjec-
tives, including participles, used as nouns [§2.6]:
etwas Neues, nichts Wichtiges; etwas Aufregendes; nichts
Bekanntes.

5.6. The "dummy subject" **es** is used like the English "there"

which is pronounced "thr:" There'll come a day when we will
regret this. The "dummy subject" postpones the real subject
of a sentence to a position after its verb. Examples: Es
war einmal ein Müller. Es steht ein Fremder vor der Tür.
Es weiß niemand, wo Gertrud jetzt wohnt.

§6. *PRINCIPAL PARTS OF VERBS*

6.1. Weak verbs

A weak verb always has a past-tense indicator -te or -ete, and a past participle ending in -t or -et. There are three categories of weak verbs.

6.1.1. Regular:

	Infinitive -en	Past tense -te	Past participle -t
Examples:	fragen	fragte	gefragt
	verursachen	verursachte	verursacht

With a verb-stem ending in t, d, fn, gn, tm:

	-en	-ete	-et
Examples:	warten	wartete	gewartet
	öffnen	öffnete	geöffnet
	verabreden	verabredete	verabredet

6.1.2. Irregular:

bringen	brachte	gebracht
denken	dachte	gedacht
brennen	brannte	gebrannt
kennen	kannte	gekannt
nennen	nannte	genannt
senden	sandte	gesandt
wenden	wandte	gewandt

The last two verbs in the above list are also used as regular weak verbs:

senden	sendete	gesendet
wenden	wendete	gewendet

There is one very irregular weak verb, with irregular present-tense forms:

Infinitive	(Present 3rd sing.)	Past tense	Past participle
wissen	(weiß)	wußte	gewußt

[For irregular present-tense forms of wissen see §7.1.1.]

6.1.3. The modal auxiliaries:

dürfen	(darf)	durfte	dürfen (gedurft)
können	(kann)	konnte	können (gekonnt)
mögen	(mag)	mochte	mögen (gemocht)
müssen	(muß)	mußte	müssen (gemußt)
sollen	(soll)	sollte	sollen (gesollt)
wollen	(will)	wollte	wollen (gewollt)

[For irregular present-tense forms of the modal auxiliaries, see §7.1.1.]

Note: The past participle forms gedurft etc. are used when there is no other verb in the infinitive form in the clause. When there is another infinitive verb — as there almost always is — the forms dürfen etc. are used.

6.2. Strong verbs

A strong verb always has a vowel difference between the forms of the present and past tenses, and its past participle ends in **-en**.

6.2.1. Most strong verbs belong to one of seven basic classes, all of which have subvarieties. All strong verbs have at least three principal parts: infinitive, first or third-person singular of the past-tense indicative, and the past participle. Some strong verbs have an additional principal part: the third-person singular of the present-tense indicative.

6.2.1.	Infinitive	Past tense	Past participle
[1a]	ei	ie	ie
	bleiben	blieb	geblieben
	(leihen, meiden, reiben, scheiden, scheinen, schreiben, schreien, schweigen, steigen, treiben, verzeihen, weisen)		
[1b]	ei	i	i
	beißen	biß	gebissen [§19.1]
	(reißen, scheißen, schmeißen)		
	gleichen	glich	geglichen
	(schleichen, streichen, weichen)		
	gleiten	glitt	geglitten
	(schreiten, streiten)		
	greifen	griff	gegriffen
	(kneifen, pfeifen, schleifen)		
	leiden	litt	gelitten
	schneiden	schnitt	geschnitten
[2a]	ie	o	o
	biegen	bog	gebogen
	(bieten, fliegen, fliehen, frieren, kriechen, riechen, schieben, verlieren, wiegen)		
	ziehen	zog	gezogen
	fließen	floß	geflossen [§19.1]
	(genießen, gießen, schießen, schließen)		
[2b]	ü	o	o
	lügen	log	gelogen
	(betrügen, trügen)		
[2c]	ö	o	o
	schwören	schwor	geschworen
[2d]	e	o	o
	heben	hob/hub	gehoben
	melken	molk	gemolken
	scheren	schor	geschoren

	Infinitive	(Present 3rd singular)	Past tense	Past participle
[2e]	e	(i)	o	o
	schmelzen	(schmilzt)	schmolz	geschmolzen
	(fechten, quellen, schwellen)			
[2f]	ö	(i)	o	o
	erlöschen	(erlischt)	erlosch	erloschen
[2g]	au	(äu)	o	o
	saufen	(säuft)	soff	gesoffen

6.2.1.

Infinitive	(Present 3rd singular)	Past tense	Past participle
[2h] au		o	o
saugen		sog	gesogen
[3a] in + cons.		an + cons.	un + cons.
binden		band	gebunden

(dringen, empfinden, finden, gelingen, klingen, ringen,
schlingen, schwingen, singen, sinken, springen, stinken,
trinken, verschwinden, winden, zwingen)

[3b] inn		ann	onn
beginnen		begann	begonnen

(gewinnen, rinnen, sinnen, spinnen)

[3c] imm		amm	omm
schwimmen		schwamm	geschwommen
[4a] e	(i)	a	e
geben	(gibt)	gab	gegeben
treten	(tritt)	trat	getreten
essen	(ißt)	aß	gegessen [§19.1]
fressen	(frißt)	fraß	gefressen [§19.1]

(messen, vergessen)

[4b] e	(ie)	a	e
lesen	(liest)	las	gelesen

(sehen, geschehen)

[4c] ie		a	e
liegen		lag	gelegen
[4d] i		a	e
bitten		bat	gebeten
sitzen		saß	gesessen
[5a] e	(i)	a	o
brechen	(bricht)	brach	gebrochen

(bergen, erschrecken, gelten, helfen, schelten, sprechen,
stechen, sterben, treffen, verderben, werben, werfen)

[5b] eh	(ieh)	ah	oh
stehlen	(stiehlt)	stahl	gestohlen

(befehlen, empfehlen)

[5c] eh	(i)	ah	o
nehmen	(nimmt)	nahm	genommen
[5d] o		a	o
kommen		kam	gekommen
[5e] ä	(ie)	a	o
gebären	(gebiert)	gebar	geboren
[6a] a	(ä)	u	a
fahren	(fährt)	fuhr	gefahren

(graben, schlagen, tragen, wachsen, waschen)

backen	(bäckt)	buk	gebacken
laden	(lädt)	lud	geladen
[6b] a		u	a
schaffen		schuf	geschaffen

6.2.1.

	Infinitive	(Present 3rd singular)	Past tense	Past participle
[7a]	a blasen	(ä) (bläst)	ie blies	a geblasen
	(braten, fallen, halten, lassen, raten, schlafen)			
[7b]	a fangen	(ä) (fängt)	i fing	a gefangen
[7c]	ä hängen		i hing	a gehangen
[7d]	ei heißen		ie hieß	ei geheißen
[7e]	o stoßen	(ö) (stößt)	ie stieß	o gestoßen
[7f]	u rufen		ie rief	u gerufen
[7g]	au laufen	(äu) (läuft)	ie lief	au gelaufen
[7h]	au hauen		ie hieb	au gehauen

6.2.2. Strong verbs which do not fit into any of the above classes:

gehen		ging	gegangen
sein	(ist)	war	gewesen
stehen		stand	gestanden
tun		tat	getan
werden	(wird)	wurde (ward)	geworden

§7. *VERB TENSES AND VERB PHRASES*

7.1. The present tense

7.1.1. Forms. The endings are:

	Singular		Plural
ich	-e	wir	-en (-n)
du	-st (-est)	ihr	-t (-et)
er/sie/es	-t (-et)	sie	-en (-n)

These endings are usually added to the infinitive stem (the infinitive without its ending -en or -n). Examples:
Infinitive: gehen, wandern; beten.
Stem: geh-, wander-/wandr-; bet-.

ich gehe, wandre; bete	wir gehen, wandern; beten
du gehst, wanderst; betest	ihr geht, wandert; betet
er geht, wandert; betet	sie gehen, wandern; beten

Variants of the infinitive stem:
Strong verbs in §6.2 for which 3rd person singular forms are given have the same vowel in the 2nd person singular. Examples:
Infinitives: sehen; fahren; laufen.
Regular infinitive stems: seh-; fahr-; lauf-.
2nd and 3rd person singular stems: sieh-; fähr-; läuf-.

ich sehe; fahre; laufe	wir sehen; fahren; laufen
du siehst; fährst; läufst	ihr seht; fahrt; lauft
er sieht; fährt; läuft	sie sehen; fahren; laufen

<u>Note</u>: Strong verbs which (1) have special 2nd and 3rd person singular stems, and (2) have stems ending in **d** or **t**, combine the final **d** or **t** with the **-t** ending of the 3rd person singular. Examples: gelten: es **gilt**; halten: er **hält**; laden: er **lädt**; raten: sie **rät**; treten: sie **tritt**.

Irregular stems and endings:
The auxiliaries **sein, haben, werden** have irregular present-tense forms:

ich bin, habe, werde	wir sind, haben, werden
du bist, hast, wirst	ihr seid, habt, werdet
er/sie/es ist, hat, wird	sie sind, haben, werden

The modal auxiliaries **dürfen, können, mögen, müssen, sollen, wollen** [§6.1.3] have regular plural forms: wir **dürfen**, ihr **dürft**, sie **dürfen**, for example; but they are irregular in the singular:

ich	darf	kann	mag	muß	soll	will
du	darfst	kannst	magst	mußt	sollst	willst
er/sie	darf	kann	mag	muß	soll	will

The verb **wissen** is similarly irregular, both as to endings and as to its stem for the singular forms:

ich weiß	wir wissen
du weißt	ihr wißt
er/sie weiß	sie wissen [§19.1]

7.1.2. Uses. The present tense is used in making statements about the present, about things or events that are true in general, and about the future when there is no chance of confusing the future with the immediate present. In narrative, the present tense is often used as a signal of an interesting or exciting new development.

7.2. The past tense

7.2.1. Forms. The endings are:

ich	—	wir	-en
du	-st (-est)	ihr	-t (-et)
er/sie/es	—	sie	-en

These endings are added directly to the past form which is the second principal part [§6].

ich sah, wartete	wir sahen, warteten
du sahst, wartetest	ihr saht, wartetet
er/sie sah, wartete	sie sahen, warteten

7.2.2. Uses. The past tense, often called the "narrative past" tense, is used in formal narratives in all parts of the German-speaking area. In conversational usage, it is commonly used in North Germany; in other parts of the German-speaking area it is generally replaced by the perfect verb phrase [§7.4] in narration about the past.

7.3. The future verb phrase

7.3.1. The present tense of **werden** [§7.1.1] + infinitive is used to make or ask for a confident statement about the future, presented as a reliable prediction. Examples:

> Was wird sein, wenn ich Meister bin? — Ja, ich werde mehr Geld verdienen, kann mir auch einen Wagen leisten, und die Mädchen werde ich zur Oberschule schicken, wenn es so weit ist... Schön wird das sein, wenn ich erst Meister bin, ich werde etwas sein...

> Es ist sicher, daß die Ergebnisse der Zellforschung für die Entwicklung der Menschheit von ebenso großer Bedeutung sein werden wie die Nutzung der Atomenergie.

> Die Folgen für das deutsche Kulturleben werden noch lange zu erkennen sein.

For the use of the present tense to indicate future time, see §7.1.2.

7.3.2. The auxiliary **werden** + infinitive can also be used to assert a probability about conditions or events in the present. Examples:

> „Wo ist Anna?" „O, sie wird wohl zu Hause sein." *(She's probably at home.)*

> Heinrich und Wolfgang werden sich besser daran erinnern als ich.

7.4. The perfect verb phrase
The present of **haben** or **sein** [§7.1.1] + the past participle of a verb.

7.4.1. **Haben** is the common auxiliary in the perfect verb phrase. It is used whenever there is a direct object in the accusative, and in most other perfect verb phrases as well. Examples:

> Ich habe heute nacht gut geschlafen. *(I slept well last night.)*

> Peter hat nicht gut geschlafen. *(Peter didn't sleep well.)*

> Gestern hab' ich einen Brief von meiner Freundin in Darmstadt bekommen. *(Yesterday I got a letter from my friend in Darmstadt.)*

> Dieser Junge hat der alten Dame über die Straße geholfen.
> *(This boy has helped the old lady across the street.)*

7.4.2. **Sein** is used as the auxiliary if
(1) there is no accusative object, AND
(2) the verb expresses a change from one position or condition to another.
Note: In addition, **sein** is the perfect auxiliary with the past participles **gewesen** (infinitive: **sein**, §6.2.2) and **geblieben** (infinitive: **bleiben**, §6.2.1[1a]).
Examples:

> Der Bus ist schon angekommen. *(The bus has already arrived.)*

> Gestern ist der Richter auf einmal krank geworden. *(Yesterday the judge suddenly became ill.)*

> Martha ist heute morgen erst um acht Uhr aufgewacht. *(Martha*

didn't wake up until eight o'clock this morning.)

Der Polizist ist dem Dieb gefolgt. *(The policeman followed the thief.)*

Im Wald ist Rotkäppchen dem bösen Wolf begegnet. *(In the woods Little Red Riding Hood met the bad wolf.)*

Note that the two "motion" verbs **folgen** and **begegnen** form the perfect verb phrase with sein. These verbs have dative objects [§1.3.2].

7.4.3. The modal auxiliaries [§6.1.3] have a special form in the perfect verb phrase. When they are used with the infinitive of another verb — as they usually are — the formula is: the present of **haben** + infinitive + **dürfen, können**, etc. (This is the so-called "double infinitive" construction. The double infinitive is the last element in a clause; it occurs even after the auxiliary in a subordinate clause.) When there is no infinitive in the clause, the perfect of a modal auxiliary has the form: **haben + gedurft, gekonnt**, etc.; this construction is quite rare. Examples of modal auxiliaries without a dependent infinitive:

Das hab' ich nie gedurft. *(I was never permitted [to do] that.)*

Arthur hat früher gut Russisch gekonnt. *(Arthur used to be able to speak Russian well.)*

Examples with the double infinitive:

Peter hat heute nacht nicht gut schlafen können. *(Peter couldn't sleep well last night.)*

Martha hat heute morgen schon um sechs Uhr aufstehen müssen. *(Martha had to get up at six o'clock this morning.)*

Martha ist heute müde, weil sie um sechs Uhr hat aufstehen müssen. *(Martha is tired today because she had to get up at six o'clock.)*

7.4.4. Uses. In informal, conversational usage, the perfect verb phrase is used to express all past action. Only in North Germany is the narrative past [§7.2] used in conversation.

Note that the perfect verb phrase is often translated into English with a simple past or the verb phrase "did + infinitive." [See examples under §7.4.1-3.]

7.5. The passive

There are several verb phrases which express a passive meaning. (Note that in the examples the words which are part of the expression illustrated are printed in "Sperrdruck" [See §19.4], and the English translation of the phrase is in Roman.)

7.5.1. The appropriate tense of verb-phrase form of **werden** + the past participle of a verb.

Present: Die Arbeit wird heute angefangen. *(The work is being started today.)*

Past: Die Arbeit wurde heute angefangen. *(The work was started yesterday.)*

Perfect: Die Arbeit ist gestern angefangen worden. *(The work was started yesterday.)*

Note the use of **sein** as the perfect auxiliary, and the special form **worden**.

Future: Die Arbeit wird morgen angefangen werden. *(The work will be started tomorrow.)*
[See also §10.3.]

7.5.2. lassen + sich + infinitive [See also §18.5.3]:

Dieses Produkt läßt sich zu Fäden ausziehen. *(This product can be drawn out to threads.)*

Das läßt sich machen. *(That can be done.)*

7.5.3. sein + zu + infinitive:

Der Schlüssel ist nicht zu finden. *(The key cannot be found.)*

Die Antwort ist auf Seite 17 zu finden. *(The answer is to be found / can be found on page 17.)*

Es ist nichts zu machen. *(Nothing can be done.)*
[For "es" see §5.6.]

7.5.4. man + inflected verb + accusative object:

Man fand das Geld in einem Schließfach. *(The money was found in a locker.)*

Bei der Herstellung des Nylons verwendet man viele Substanzen. *(Many substances are used in the manufacture of nylon.)*

7.5.5. Subject referring to something inanimate + inflected verb + sich:

Das Geld wird sich gewiß schon wieder finden. *(Surely the money will be found.)*

Der Vorgang wiederholt sich dauernd. *(The process is constantly repeated.)*

7.6. Subjunctive I (the "quotative")
7.6.1. Forms. The following endings are added to the regular infinitive stem [§7.1.1]:

ich	-e	wir	-en
du	-est	ihr	-et
er/sie	-e	sie	-en

Examples: ich **wisse**, du **wissest**, er/sie **wisse**; ich **dürfe**, sie **könne**, etc.; er **sehe**; sie **werfe**; du **tragest**; sie **schließe**.
The verb **sein** has special subjunctive I forms:

ich sei	wir seien
du seiest	ihr seiet
er sei	sie seien

Note: If subjunctive I forms are identical with present-tense indicative forms, e.g. wir **wissen**, ich **sehe**, sie **können**, subjunctive II forms must be used [§7.7].

7.6.2. Uses
7.6.2.1. Subjunctive I is used chiefly in quoting the statements

or questions of someone not the speaker or writer.
[See §12.]

7.6.2.2. It is frequently used with the idiomatic expression
als ob. [See also §7.7.2.4 and §11.5.]

7.6.2.3. It is sometimes used in the directions for scientific
experiments and in cooking recipes:
> **Man nehme ein Pfund Kartoffeln...**

7.7. Subjunctive II

7.7.1. Forms. Subjunctive II verb forms have the same <u>endings</u>
as subjunctive I [§7.6.1]; however, the <u>stems</u> are different. Subjunctive II stems are closely related to the
past-tense stems [see principal parts, §6].

7.7.1.1. Weak verbs:

7.7.1.1.1. Regular weak verbs [§6.1.1] have identical forms in
the past-tense indicative and in subjunctive II.

7.7.1.1.2. Irregular weak verbs [§6.1.2] have the following stems:
brächt-, dächt-, brennt-, kennt-, etc., **wüßt-.**

7.7.1.1.3. Modal auxiliaries [§6.1.3] have the following stems:
dürft-, könnt-, möcht-, müßt-, sollt-, wollt-.

7.7.1.2. The auxiliaries **haben, sein, werden** have the subjunctive
II stems **hätt-, wär-, würd-.**

7.7.1.3. Strong verbs:

7.7.1.3.1. If the past-tense stem contains the vowel **i** or **ie,** the
subjunctive II stem is identical with the past-tense
stem. Examples:

Past tense	Subjunctive II
sie blieb	sie bliebe
er fing...an	er finge...an

7.7.1.3.2. If the past-tense stem contains **a, o, u,** the corresponding subjunctive II stem contains **ä, ö, ü.**
Examples:

ich band	ich bände
er schoß	er schösse
sie fuhr	sie führe

7.7.1.3.3. Exceptions:

half	hülfe
starb	stürbe
warf	würfe
stand	stünde

7.7.2. Uses

7.7.2.1. In quoting statements or questions, where the subjunctive
I forms are identical with indicative forms [§7.6.1:Note].

7.7.2.2. For softened statements, orders, or requests:
> **Das hätte ich nicht sagen sollen. Könnten Sie mir sagen,...?
> Dürfte ich bitten?**

7.7.2.3. In conditional sentences: unreal conditions and conditions contrary to fact [§11.2, 11.3].

7.7.2.4. It is frequently used with the idiomatic expression **als
ob:**
> **Er tat, als ob er nichts gehört hätte.**

[See also §7.6.2.2 and §11.5.]

7.8. Modal auxiliary verb phrases

7.8.1. Forms

7.8.1.1. The modal auxiliaries are: **dürfen, können, mögen, müssen, sollen, wollen.** They are almost always used with a dependent infinitive (<u>not</u> preceded by **zu**). Example:

>   Der Fabrikarbeiter muß jeden morgen um 5:30 aufstehen.

> [For principal parts see §6.1.3; for present-tense forms, §7.1.1; for the perfect verb phrase §7.4.3.]

7.8.1.2. The infinitive of a motion verb is omitted when a goal or destination is otherwise expressed in the sentence:

>   Mein Mann muß noch zur Post. (=zur Post gehen)
>   Nun muß ich aber an die Arbeit.

7.8.1.3. The modal auxiliaries **können** and **mögen** are occasionally used with a direct object:

>   Der Direktor kann etwas Englisch, aber er spricht es nicht fließend. *(The manager can speak some English, but he doesn't speak it fluently.)*

>   Mögen Sie Hunde? *(Do you like dogs?)*

>   Ich mag kein Frühstück. *(I don't want any breakfast.)*

7.8.2. Meanings. The modal auxiliaries are etymologically related to the modal auxiliaries in English (can, dare, may, must, shall, will); but they most often cannot be translated with the related English verb. Examples:

7.8.2.1. dürfen

>   Darf ich mich vorstellen? *(May I introduce myself?)*

>   Das darfst du nicht sagen. *(You mustn't say that.)*

>   Lise darf tun, was sie will. *(It's all right for Lise to do what she wants to.)*

7.8.2.2. können

>   Ich kann jetzt wieder gehen. *(I can walk again now.)*

>   Der Präsident allein kann keinen Krieg erklären. *(The President on his own authority cannot [does not have the power to] declare war.)*

7.8.2.3. mögen

>   Ich mag ihn nicht leiden. *(I can't stand him.)*

>   Er mag sagen, was er will, er ist trotzdem schuld daran. *(He can say what he wants, he is nonetheless guilty.)*

>   Lise mag tun, was sie will. *(Lise is capable of doing whatever she wants to.)*

>   Herr Keller mag etwa vierzig Jahre alt sein. *(Mr. Keller is probably about forty years old.)*

>   Ich möchte lieber nicht darauf eingehen. *(I would rather not discuss that.)*

7.8.2.4. müssen

>   Als Heinz mit seinem neuen Sportwagen eine Probefahrt machte,

da mußte plötzlich ein Polizist aus dem Nichts erscheinen.
(When Hank was trying out his new sports car, fate would have it that suddenly a patrolman appeared out of nowhere.)

Mußt du denn alles wissen?   *(Do you have to know everything?)*

Die kleine Inge mußte nicht zu Bett gehen.   *(Little Inge didn't have to go to bed.)*

7.8.2.5. sollen

Was soll ich tun?   *(What am I supposed to do?)*

Du sollst nicht töten.   *(Exodus 20, 13)*

Ihr hättet zu uns kommen sollen.   *(You should have come to our place.)*

Viele sollen an diesem Tag umgekommen sein.   *(Many are said to have perished on that day.)*

Der neue Nachbar soll reich sein.   *(They say that the new neighbor is rich.)*

Verbrechen, die er begangen haben soll,...   *(crimes he is alleged to have committed...)*

7.8.2.6. wollen

Mein Bruder will, daß ich mitgehe.   *(My brother wants me to go along.)*

Ich will morgen abreisen.   *(I'm planning to start my trip tomorrow.)*

Der Bürgermeister wollte eben ausgehen, als ich kam. *(The mayor was just about to leave when I came.)*

Die Uhr wollte eben schlagen.   *(The clock was about to strike.)*

Das will gelernt sein.   *(That's something you have to learn.)*

Ich will nicht!   *(I don't want to!)*

Das will ich nicht gehört haben.   *(I'll claim that I didn't hear that. = You shouldn't have said that.)*

Der neue Nachbar will reich sein.   *(He claims that he is rich.)*

Der neue Nachbar will reich werden.   *(He wants to get rich.)*

§8. *THE POSITION OF THE VERB*

8.1. The inflected verb, that is, that verb form which agrees with the subject of the sentence, is regularly the second element in the main clause.

8.1.1. "Normal word order:" The first element is a noun phrase or pronoun in the nominative case, the subject.
(Note that in the following example sentences the subject is underlined, the verb is indicated with "Sperrdruck" [§19.4].)

Chlor verbindet sich leicht mit anderen Elementen.

Wir wohnen Lessingstraße achtzehn.

8.1.2. "Inverted word order:" Some element of the sentence other than the subject is emphasized by being placed before the subject and inflected verb. The "normal" order of subject + verb is then "inverted," and the word order is usually: sentence element which is not the subject + inflected verb + subject. Occasionally the sequence of verb + subject is interrupted by an intervening

pronoun object:

> Im Krankenhaus besuchten ihn sämtliche Mitglieder des Singvereins.

> Mit leisen Tritten sind ihm die beiden Detektive gefolgt.

sentence adverbial expression:

> In einem Gebiet leben stets mehr Pflanzen- als Fleischfresser.

> Da ging auf einmal die Tür auf.

prepositional phrase:

> Beim Pferd sind statt der Nagezähne Schneidezähne ausgebildet.

> Vielleicht werden in den kommenden Jahrzehnten bessere Desinfektionsmittel in den Trinkwasseranlagen der Städte benutzt werden.

The sentence element which is placed before the verb + subject sequence may be

8.1.2.1. a noun phrase or a pronoun in the accusative case:

> Eine Antwort konnte ich ihr nicht geben.

8.1.2.2. a noun phrase or a pronoun in the dative case:

> Unserem Hund gefällt die neue Wohnung.

> Mir hat Monika nichts davon gesagt.

8.1.2.3. an adverb:

> Leider haben wir keine Bananen mehr.

8.1.2.4. a prepositional phrase:

> Mit seinen Nagezähnen zerkleinert der Hase harte Pflanzenstoffe.

8.1.2.5. a past participle, an infinitive, or the separable part of a compound verb, usually found at the end of the clause:

> Beschreiben kann man die Farbe nicht. [§7.8.1.1]

> Unterstützt werden sie dabei durch die Militaristen. [§7.5.1]

> Auf tut sich der Zwinger. [§9.5.1]

8.1.2.6. a subordinate clause:

> Bevor Herr Behnke zu Abend ißt, liest er die Zeitung.

Note: In a conditional sentence with the condition stated first, so or dann is often used before the inflected verb of the independent clause:

Wenn Frau Straub sich etwas vorgenommen hat, dann führt
<u>sie</u> es auch aus.

Hätte Herr Fenske dabei sein können, so hätten <u>wir</u> diese
Schwierigkeiten nicht.

8.2. "Initial verb" order: The inflected verb is the first
element in

8.2.1. imperative sentences:

Bringen Sie mir, bitte, ein Glas Bier.

8.2.2. "Yes/No" questions:

Kannst du schwimmen?

8.2.3. the condition (the "if"-clause) of a conditional sentence
if wenn is omitted [see also §11.4]:

Sucht man eine Verbindung immer weiter zu unterteilen, so
kommt man zu einer bestimmten, endlichen Grenze.

8.2.4. an idiom with **doch** following the subject:

Ist Professor Doktor Gautzsch doch ein berühmter Chemiker.
(But after all, Professor Gautzsch is a famous chemist!)

8.2.5. poetry, imitating older styles:

Sah ein Knab' ein Röslein stehn. *(A lad saw a little rose.)*

8.3. With "normal," "inverted," and "initial verb" order, all
other forms associated with the inflected verb — infinitives, past participles, and the separable components of
compound verbs [§9.5.1] — are found at or near the end of
the clause. [See also §8.1.2.5.]
(In the following examples, the associated element is
printed in "Sperrdruck" [§19.4].)

Im Laufe der Entwicklung sind die Klassenunterschiede
verschwunden.

Soll sie hingehen   und ihren eigenen Mann anzeigen?

Note, however, the position of the infinitive in the following:

Monikas Bruder Klaus wird wohl jünger sein als sie.
[§7.3.2]

8.4. "Subordinate word order:" In subordinate clauses the inflected verb is at the end of the clause unless followed
by an expression added as an afterthought. There are
five main types of subordinate clauses:

8.4.1. Subordinate clauses introduced by subordinating conjunctions, e.g. als, bevor, da, damit, ehe, indem, nachdem,
während, weil.

8.4.1.1. The subordinating conjunctions als, ob, wenn, wann are
often confusing.

8.4.1.1.1. Als is used to introduce a single past action and is
translated into English as "when." [§18.1.1]

Als das Mädchen zu ihm gebracht wurde, führte er es in eine

Kammer voll Stroh. *(When the girl was brought to him, he led her into a chamber full of straw.)*

8.4.1.1.2. Ob is used to make an indirect question out of a direct question beginning with the verb. [§8.2.2] It is translated into English as "whether, if." [See also §12.1.3.]

Ich frage mich, ob ich wirklich krank bin. *(I wonder whether I am really sick.)*

8.4.1.1.3. Wann is used as a subordinating conjunction only in an indirect question formed from a direct question with **wann.** [See also §12.1.1.]

Ich weiß nicht, wann der Zug ankommen soll. *(I don't know when the train is supposed to arrive.)*

8.4.1.1.4. Wenn is used (a) in a conditional clause [see §11]; (b) in a clause expressing repeated action in the past.

Wenn das Kind zum Zahnarzt gehen mußte, schrie es immer. *(Whenever the child had to go to the dentist, it always screamed.)*

8.4.1.2. Note also **indem:** When the subject of a subordinate clause introduced by **indem** is the same as the subject of the main clause, **indem** + verb can be translated into English: (by) + verb + -ing.

Du kannst ihm eine Freude bereiten, indem du ihn einmal besuchst. *(You can give him pleasure by visiting him some time.)*

8.4.2. Question words (for example, **wo, wie, warum, wann, was, wer, wem**) can function as conjunctions to introduce subordinate clauses. [See §12.1.1.]

8.4.3. The condition (the "if-clause") in a conditional sentence is a subordinate clause. [See §11.]

8.4.4. Indirect discourse often takes the form of a subordinate clause. [See §12.]

8.4.5. A relative clause is always a subordinate clause. [See §13.]

§9. *WORD FORMATION*

German has a number of prefixes and suffixes, many of which indicate the meaning or the function of a word in a sentence.

9.1. Noun suffixes
9.1.1. Neuter
9.1.1.1. **-chen, -lein:** Mädchen, Männlein (diminutives or terms of endearment: Liebchen)
9.1.1.2. **-tel:** Drittel, Viertel, Achtel, Hundertstel (fractions)
9.1.1.3. **-tum:** Christentum, Eigentum (abstract terms)
        Note: **der Irrtum, der Reichtum**

9.1.2. Feminine
9.1.2.1. **-in:** Lehrerin, Studentin, Löwin, Beamtin
9.1.2.2. **-heit, -keit:** Christenheit, Menschheit (noun + -heit =

large collection); Freiheit, Verrücktheit (adjective +
-heit = quality). Note: **-keit** is added to adjectives
ending in **-bar**, **-ig**, **-lich**, **-sam** [§9.2]: Freundlichkeit,
Sparsamkeit.

9.1.2.3. **-erei**: Malerei, Spielerei, Bäckerei (verb + **-erei** =
activity, or place where activity takes place; sometimes
has a derogatory sense: Schreiberei - a lot of useless
scribbling)

9.1.2.4. **-schaft**: Hörerschaft, Verwandtschaft, Bekanntschaft
(noun + **-schaft** = a group or collection; adjective +
-schaft = a general quality)

9.1.2.5. **-ung**: Ernennung, Entfernung, Gewinnung (infinitive stem
+ **-ung** = action or abstraction)

9.1.2.6. **-e**: Gabe, Sprache, Ehre, Lehre (verb form + **-e**); Größe,
Länge, Breite (adjective + **¨e/-e**)

9.1.3. Masculine:

9.1.3.1. **-er**, **-ler**, **-ner**: Fahrer, Tischler, Gärtner (agent nouns)

9.1.3.2. **-ling**: Jüngling, Liebling, Flüchtling, Steckling (young,
immature, or helpless people, animals, or plants)
[See also §2.2-6.]

9.2. Adjective suffixes

9.2.1. **-bar**: lesbar, denkbar, furchtbar, trinkbar (about like
-able/-ible in English: suitable for, capable of)

9.2.2. **-fähig**: flugfähig, lebensfähig, sprachfähig (capable of)

9.2.3. **-haft**, **-ig**, **-lich**: spaßhaft, anekdotenhaft; zweiseitig,
zeitig, dreijährig, heißblütig; kindlich, ehrlich, ge-
fährlich

9.2.4. **-isch**: amerikanisch, italienisch, vaterländisch; philo-
sophisch, logisch; kindisch, äffisch (countries / nouns
of foreign extraction + **-isch** = adjective; but when used
with nouns of German origin it has a derogatory sense:
kindlich - childlike; kindisch - childish; äffisch
[from "Affe"] - apish, silly)

9.2.5. **-los**: endlos, leblos (**-less**)

9.2.6. **-mäßig**: regelmäßig, zeitmäßig (according to, appropriate
for)

9.2.7. **-sam**: langsam, einsam, furchtsam (having a quality or
property)

9.2.8. **-d**: liebend, lachend (infinitive + **-d** = present participle, used only as adjective or adverb)
[For nominalizations of adjectives, see §2.6.]

9.3. Verb suffixes

(Note: Verbs with these suffixes are always weak [§6.1.1.])

9.3.1. **-igen**: steinigen, ängstigen, einigen (noun/adjective +
-igen = verb)

9.3.2. **-eln**: lächeln, kränkeln (diminutive); betteln, schmuggeln

9.3.3. **-ieren**, **-isieren**, **-eien**: buchstabieren, halbieren; mo-
dernisieren, tyrannisieren; prophezeien, benedeien
(most often used to Germanize verbs of foreign origin:
e.g. boykottieren, objektivieren)
Note: Verbs ending in **-ieren**, **-isieren**, **-eien** have no
ge- in the past participle. They have the stress on the
-ier-/-ei- syllable in all forms.

9.4. Noun and adjective prefixes

9.4.1. **Erz-, erz-:** Erzbischof, Erzsäufer; erzdumm, erzfaul
(arch-, extreme: Erzbösewicht - archvillain)

9.4.2. **Un-, un-:** unwichtig, unwohl (negation); Unglück, Unkraut
(something bad or evil); Ungeheuer, Unmenge (something
enormously large); Undank, Ungeschmack (lack of something)
Note: This prefix has such a variety of functions that
it is wise to check any uncertainty.

9.4.3. **Ur-:** Ursache, Urwald, Urmensch, Ursprung (original, pri-
meval; but not Urlaub - vacation, leave)

9.5. Compound and prefixed verbs

9.5.1. Compound ("separable") verbs. These consist of a true
verb and an associated word. The associated word is a
word in its own right: one of the common prepositions
like **an, auf, aus, bei, mit, nach, vor, zu** or an adverb
like **ab, weg, zusammen, hin, hindurch, her, hervor, ein**
(as an adverb, **ein** has the meaning "in, into"). The associated element is independent, in that it has its own
position in the clause: it occurs at or near the end.
Accordingly it occurs along with the true-verb part of
the compound only when that true-verb component is at
the end of the clause, that is, when it is an infinitive
or a participle or the final word in a subordinate clause.
Under these conditions, the compound is written as a con-
tinuous string of letters. The **ge-** of the past participle comes at its usual place at the beginning of the true-
verb part. The same thing is true in the construction
zu + infinitive: aus**zu**sehen, ein**zu**laden, mit**zu**machen.

The principal parts of compound separable verbs are
written:

Infinitive	(Present 3rd singular)	Past tense	Past participle
aussehen	(sieht...aus)	sah...aus	ausgesehen
einladen	(lädt...ein)	lud...ein	eingeladen
mitmachen	(macht...mit)	machte...mit	mitgemacht

Note: In spoken German the stress is on the separable
word: **aus**sehen, **ein**geladen, **mit**machen. The separable
word usually retains some of its own meaning, as would
be expected in an element which has its own position in
the clause and has the stress. Many of the compound
verbs, especially those formed with **hin** (often meaning
"away from the speaker") and **her** ("toward the speaker")
and their many combinations with prepositions: **hinüber,
heran, hervor,** etc., are not listed in the dictionary.

9.5.2. Prefixed verbs. Several prefix-syllables are used with
root verbs: **be-, emp-, ent-, er-, ge-, miß-, ver-, zer-.**
These prefixes are never separated from the verb (they
are often called the "inseparable prefixes"). They have
much less definite meanings than the "separable" verbs.
With them, there is no **ge-** participial prefix. These
prefixes do not have the stress in spoken German.

Following are a few examples of principal parts of prefixed verbs:

Infinitive	(Present 3rd singular)	Past tense	Past participle
bedienen	(bedient)	bediente	bedient
enthalten	(enthält)	enthielt	enthalten
mißlingen	(mißlingt)	mißlang	mißlungen

Note: Some of these prefixes, especially **be-** and **ver-**, often have the effect of making verbs out of nouns or adjectives. Notice the following:

Ehre: beehren	mehr: vermehren
Kleid: bekleiden	schön: verschönen
Neid: beneiden	schöner: verschönern
Schmutz: beschmutzen	Ursache: verursachen

All verbs of this type are weak:

beschmutzen	(beschmutzt)	beschmutzte	beschmutzt
verursachen	(verursacht)	verursachte	verursacht
beneiden	(beneidet)	beneidete	beneidet

9.5.3. durch, über, um, unter, wider

These words are sometimes used as prefixes, sometimes as the separable part of a compound verb. When they are the separable element in a compound verb, they usually have an approximately literal meaning; as "inseparable" prefixes they give the verb a more figurative meaning. Sometimes it happens that one of these words is used either separably or inseparably with the same root verb, with two very different meanings:

über_setzen_	(über_setzt_)	über_setzte_	über_setzt_
_über_setzen	(setzt..._über_)	setzte..._über_	_über_gesetzt

(über_setzen_ - *translate*; _über_setzen - *carry across [in a ferry]*)

durch_brechen_	(durch_bricht_)	durch_brach_	durch_brochen_
_durch_brechen	(bricht..._durch_)	brach..._durch_	_durch_gebrochen

(durch_brechen_ - *penetrate*; _durch_brechen - *break in two, break through*)

§10. *WERDEN*

The verb **werden** has four uses: a) as an independent verb meaning "get, become;" b) as the auxiliary indicating the future; c) as the auxiliary indicating the passive; d) in the form **würd-**, as an auxiliary in unreal and contrary-to-fact conditions. The first three of these will be discussed below. For the last, see §11.2 and §11.3.

10.1. The independent verb may occur in the present, past, future (wird...werden), perfect (ist...geworden), pluperfect (war...geworden), future perfect (wird...geworden sein). (But note that the future perfect is a rare form in any verb.) The independent verb **werden** is easily recognized by the lack of any other verb dependent on it.

> Es ist sehr selten, daß Nachbarn Freunde werden. (*It is very rare that neighbors become friends.*)

> Die Katze ist zum Streicheltier geworden. (*The cat has become a pet.*)

Note: The form **geworden** indicates the independent verb.

10.2. The two characteristics of the <u>future verb phrase</u> are:
1) the auxiliary **werden** is always in the present tense;
2) there is always an infinitive within the same clause
[§7.3.1].

> Wir können gespannt sein, wann wir wieder Luftschiffe sehen
> werden. *(We can look forward eagerly to the time when we'll
> see airships again.)*

10.3. The passive verb phrase
10.3.1. The <u>passive verb phrase</u> is distinguished by the use of
the past participle with the verb **werden** [§7.5.1].

> Present: Chlor wird zum Bleichen benutzt.
> Die Gräser werden von der Kuh mit dem breiten Maul und
> der auffällig langen Zunge abgerupft.
>
> Past: Nylon wurde im Jahre 1938 auf den Markt gebracht.
>
> Perfect: Im Zweiten Weltkrieg ist die Schweiz verschont worden.
>
> With a modal auxiliary:
> Nach dem Abkühlen konnten die Fäden noch weiter gestreckt
> werden.

Note: When **worden** occurs (see the example for the perfect above), it is a clear sign of the passive.

10.3.2. Agent and instrument. **Von** + dative indicates the person
or persons involved as the cause of the process or situation described in a passive sentence.

> Egon Witte wurde von seinem Chef gelobt. *(Egon Witte was
> praised by his boss.)*

Durch + accusative indicates the impersonal force, tool,
condition, etc. because of which or by means of which
the process or situation is produced.

> Der Bahnhof wurde durch Bomben zerstört. *(The railroad station
> was destroyed by bombs.)*
>
> Europa wird von Afrika durch das Mittelmeer getrennt. *(Europe
> is separated from Africa by the Mediterranean.)*
>
> Der General wurde durch einen Boten vom Sieg benachrichtigt.
> *(The general was notified of the victory by [by means of] a
> messenger.)*

Note that this distinction between agent and instrument
is not made in English, that both can be expressed in a
prepositional phrase with "by."

10.3.3. Dative object
10.3.3.1. Many sentences in the active have two objects — direct
and indirect, in the accusative and dative respectively.
The dative case form is used unchanged in a corresponding passive sentence.

> Active: Heinz gab dem Mädchen einen Kuß.
>
> Passive: Dem Mädchen wurde von Heinz ein Kuß gegeben.

10.3.3.2. Some verbs have only a dative object [see §1.3.2].
This dative object form is also used unchanged in a
corresponding passive sentence:

Active: Man kann dem armen alten Weib nicht helfen.

Passive: Dem armen alten Weib kann nicht geholfen werden.

In short: "Dative remains dative."

§11. CONDITIONAL SENTENCES

A conditional sentence is divided into two parts: the condition, usually introduced by the subordinating conjunction "if" in English, **wenn** in German; and the main statement or consequence of the condition. These two parts may occur in either order.

11.1. "Real" conditions. The condition of a "real" conditional sentence <u>can</u> be fulfilled. The grammatical clue to a "real" conditional sentence is that the verbs are always in the indicative.

> *We'll go for a long walk if it doesn't rain.*

> *If I have enough money, I'll get you a radio for your birthday.*

> Wenn Sie morgen Zeit haben, können Sie vielleicht zu mir kommen.

"Real" conditions can also be in the past:

Present: Wenn wir mit Lufthansa fliegen, dann kommen wir am nächsten Morgen in Frankfurt an.

Past: Wenn wir mit Lufthansa flogen, dann kamen wir am nächsten Morgen in Frankfurt an.

Note: These real conditions in the past are usually expressed in English with "whenever" instead of "if."

11.2. "Unreal" conditions. It is unlikely that the condition of an "unreal" conditional sentence will be fulfilled. The grammatical clue is that the verbs are in the subjunctive.

> *If I had the money right now (but I don't), I'd get you a radio for your birthday right now (but I can't).*

Note: Although the verb form is the same as the past indicative, it denotes the present. This use of the past form to express present time is the only clue with most English verbs that the form is a subjunctive. Only the verb "be" has a subjunctive form different from the indicative:

> *If he were not so tall (but he is very tall), he would not be playing basketball.*

Note that the form "he were" is not a standard indicative past form.

In German the "unreal" condition also has a subjunctive in both the **wenn**-clause and the main clause. Only subjunctive II [§7.7] is used in conditional sentences.

> Wenn wir fliegen könnten, so würden wir morgen ankommen.

> Alles würde besser gehen, wenn man mehr zu Fuß ginge.

In modern usage verbs which have a vowel change in the subjunctive II (**sah - sähe; flog - flöge; fuhr - führe**) are paraphrased to avoid the pure subjunctive form. Most commonly a verb phrase with **würd-** or the subjunctive of one of the modal auxiliaries: **dürft-, könnt-**, etc., is substituted for the subjunctive of the main verb, which sounds old-fashioned and stiff. A sentence like the following sounds stilted:

> Wenn die Autofahrer langsamer führen, sparten sie Benzin.

It might be paraphrased thus:

> Wenn die Autofahrer langsamer fahren wollten, würden sie Benzin sparen.

11.3. "Contrary-to-fact" conditions. The condition of the "contrary-to-fact" conditional sentence can never be fulfilled, because everything is in the past. The grammatical clue is that the verbs are in the past subjunctive. Remember: the only way to express past time in the subjunctive is with **hätt-/wär-** + past participle.

> Wenn die Königin Rumpelstilzchens Namen nicht entdeckt hätte, hätte sie ihm ihr Kind geben müssen. *(If the queen hadn't discovered Rumpelstiltskin's name, she would have had to give him her child.)*

Notice the relationship of these forms:

Real condition:	Wenn er vorsichtig ist, so passiert ihm das nicht. *(If he is careful, that won't happen to him.)*
Unreal condition:	Wenn er vorsichtig wäre, so würde ihm das nicht passieren. *(If he were careful, that wouldn't happen to him.)*
Contrary-to-fact:	Wenn er vorsichtig gewesen wäre, so wäre ihm das nicht passiert. *(If he had been careful, that wouldn't have happened to him.)*

11.4. The word **wenn** may be omitted in any one of the three types of conditional sentences. When it is omitted, the verb of the conditional clause is in the initial position. (Compare English: "Had I known that,..." = "If I had known that,...")

> Hätte die Königin Rumpelstilzchens Namen nicht entdeckt, dann hätte sie ihm ihr erstes Kind geben müssen.

Or:

> Die Königin hätte Rumpelstilzchen ihr erstes Kind geben müssen, hätte sie seinen Namen nicht entdeckt.

> Wäre er vorsichtig, so würde ihm das nicht passieren.

> Fliegen wir mit Lufthansa, dann kommen wir am nächsten Morgen in Frankfurt an.

11.5. The phrases "as if, as though" are expressed in German by **als ob, als wenn**. These expressions are followed by subjunctive, either subjunctive I or II.

> Er tat, als ob er ein feiner Herr sei. *(He acted as though he were an aristocrat.)*

> Sie tat, als wenn sie meine Worte nicht gehört hätte.

In sentences like the above, **ob** or **wenn** can be omitted. In case of this omission, the verb follows **als**.

> Er tat, als hätte er meine Worte nicht gehört.

> Es kam mir vor, als hörte ich eine fremde Sprache.

§12. *DIRECT AND INDIRECT DISCOURSE*

12.1. Imagine that an employee (der Angestellte) has his superior (der Chef) on the telephone and is conducting an interview according to the latter's orders.

> Der Chef: Fragen Sie ihn, <u>wie</u> er heißt.
> Der Angestellte (zum Mann): <u>Wie</u> heißen Sie, bitte? [§12.1.1]

> Der Mann: Ich heiße Schmidt.
> Der Angestellte (ins Telephon): Er sagt, er heißt Schmidt. [§12.1.2]

> Der Chef: Das glaube ich nicht. Fragen Sie ihn, <u>ob</u> er nicht wirklich Weizenegger heißt.
> Der Angestellte (zum Mann): Heißen Sie nicht wirklich Weizenegger? [§12.1.3]

> Der Mann: Nein, ich heiße Schmidt.
> Der Angestellte (ins Telephon): Er besteht darauf, <u>daß</u> er Schmidt heißt. [§12.1.4]

> Der Chef: Na, dann sagen Sie ihm, <u>daß</u> er zu mir kommen soll.
> Der Angestellte (zum Mann): Der Chef glaubt Ihnen nicht. Er will persönlich mit Ihnen sprechen. Gehen Sie, bitte, zu ihm. Sein Büro ist hier nebenan. [§12.1.5]

12.1.1. When a direct question with a question-word is stated as an indirect question, the question-word is the connective and functions as a subordinating conjunction. Thus the inflected verb is in the final position [§8.4.2].

> Direct: <u>Warum</u> antworten Sie nicht?
> Indirect: Fragen Sie die Frau, <u>warum</u> sie nicht antwortet.

12.1.2. The man answers:

> Ich heiße Schmidt.

The clerk reports:

> Er sagt, er heißt Schmidt.

The clerk could just as well have said:

> Er sagt, <u>daß</u> er Schmidt heißt.

Notice the two possible positions of the verb, with or without the subordinating conjunction **daß**.

12.1.3. The indirect counterpart of a "Yes/No" question, that is, a question beginning with a verb, is introduced by the subordinating conjunction **ob**.

> Direct: Willst du mitgehen?
> Indirect: Jürgen weiß nicht, <u>ob</u> er mitgehen will.

12.1.4. The indirect statement is sometimes introduced by a phrase consisting of a verb + da-compound: **Er besteht darauf ... sie denkt daran ... wir sprechen davon ...** After such a construction **daß** cannot be omitted, as it was in the second exchange above. [See also §17.1.2.]

12.1.5. The boss gives an indirect command:

> Sagen Sie ihm, <u>daß</u> er zu mir kommen soll.

The clerk transfers this command to the man:

> Gehen Sie, bitte, zu ihm.

The indirect command is expressed with the modal auxiliary **sollen.**

Direct: Lesen Sie diese Geschichte bis Montag durch. *(Finish reading this story by Monday.)*

Indirect: Sagen Sie den Studenten, sie sollen diese Geschichte bis Montag durchlesen / <u>daß</u> sie ... durchlesen sollen.

12.2. The above treatment of indirect discourse demonstrates its use in a conversational situation, when direct questions, statements, and commands are expressed indirectly in the indicative form of the verb. However, when indirect discourse is used formally, in a narrative, or when a newspaper reporter or a TV commentator is quoting a source, the indirect quotation is in the subjunctive. [§7.6 and §7.7]

The most frequently encountered form of the quotative subjunctive is the third-person singular. This third-person singular of the subjunctive is <u>always</u> a different form from the indicative. Study the following pairs, the first of which is the indicative, the second, subjunctive I: macht/mache; will/wolle; hat/habe; wird/werde; heißt/heiße; kommt/komme; hält/halte. It should also be noted that even when a subjunctive I form is available (that is, the subjunctive I form is different from the indicative), the subjunctive II form is sometimes used.

> Der Schwimmeister Spitz sagte: „Ich bin damit zufrieden."
> Spitz sagte, er sei damit zufrieden / er wäre damit zufrieden.

12.3. If the direct discourse is in the present tense, the formal form of the indirect discourse is in the present subjunctive I or II, as in the following table:

	Indicative	Subjunctive I	Subjunctive II
Present	er weiß es kommt...an	er wisse es komme...an	er wüßte es käme...an

12.4. If the direct discourse is in past time (simple past tense, present perfect, or past perfect), the indirect discourse must be in the perfect subjunctive I or II.

	er wußte er hat...gewußt er hatte...gewußt	er habe...gewußt	er hätte...gewußt
Past	es kam...an es ist...angekommen es war...angekommen	es sei...angekommen	es wäre...angekommen

12.5. The future also has two possible forms:

Future	er wird...kommen	er werde...kommen	er würde...kommen

§13. *RELATIVE CLAUSES*

13.1. One of the important skills in reading or listening to
German is the instant and accurate recognition of the
definite article, the emphatic pronoun, and the relative
pronoun, which have similar forms. Review §4.1 and §5.2.

13.1.1. The <u>relative pronoun</u> comes at the beginning of a subordinate clause — and the verb in a subordinate clause
is always at the end. The relative pronoun normally refers to the last noun with which it agrees in gender and
number.

> Der Mann in der Ecke, den ich nicht kenne...

The relative pronoun **den**, a masculine form, must refer
to the noun **Mann**. The statement:

> Die Frau in der Ecke, die ich nicht sehen kann...

could be ambiguous, because the pronoun **die** might refer
to either **Frau** or **Ecke**.

13.1.2. The <u>emphatic pronoun</u> is the stressed form of the personal pronoun. The third-person personal pronouns [§5.1]
will not take much stress in speech. When the accent
falls on the pronoun, the speaker generally uses the
emphatic rather than the personal pronoun.

> Not: Du sprichst von Lieselotte. Aber sie ist meine Freundin!

> But: Du sprichst von Lieselotte. Aber die ist meine Freundin!

(The stressed forms are printed in "Sperrdruck" [§19.4].)

Another characteristic of the emphatic pronoun is that
it usually occurs toward the beginning of a clause.
Note the difference in position:

> Ich habe ihn heute nicht gesehen. (<u>ihn</u> *unstressed*)
> Den hab' ich heute nicht gesehen. (<u>den</u> *stressed*)

13.1.3. The <u>definite article</u> is always followed by either an
adjective or a noun or an adjective-noun phrase. [But
see also §14.] One situation is potentially confusing:
when a relative pronoun is followed by a noun phrase,
for example:

> Der Lehrer, der kluge Schüler in seiner Klasse hat, ist
> wirklich glücklich.

One might take **der kluge Schüler** for a noun phrase headed
by a definite article, but the verb at the end of the
subordinate clause indicates that **der** is a relative pronoun referring to **Lehrer**; **kluge Schüler** is accusative
plural [§3.4 and §4.7].

13.2. An independent sentence can be made out of a relative
clause by putting the verb in the second position and using
instead of the relative pronoun either: a) the corresponding personal pronoun (in the case of the genitive, the

corresponding possessive adjective), or b) the noun to
which the relative pronoun refers. Examples:

13.2.1. Die alte Dame, der du über die Straße geholfen hast, ist dir
dankbar.
     a) Du hast ihr über die Straße geholfen.
     b) Du hast der alten Dame über die Straße geholfen.

13.2.2. Meine Freundin, deren Zensuren immer gut sind, ist doch auch
intelligent.
     a) Ihre Zensuren sind immer gut.
     b) Die Zensuren meiner Freundin sind immer gut.

13.2.3. Das Gebäude, dessen Fassade erneuert wird, ist ein Warenhaus.
     a) Seine Fassade wird erneuert.
     b) Die Fassade des Gebäudes wird erneuert.

13.2.4. Der Anzug, an dem ein Knopf fehlt, muß in die Reinigung.
     a) An ihm (daran) fehlt ein Knopf. [daran: §17.1.1]
     b) Am Anzug fehlt ein Knopf.

13.3. The opposite process is the synthesis of two sentences,
the second of which has a pronoun or a possessive referring to a noun in the first, into one sentence with a
relative clause. This is done in the following steps:

13.3.1. Replace the pronoun or possessive with a relative pronoun, using the pronoun tables in §5. Note that no
matter what ending the possessive adjective **sein** may
have: **seine, seinen, seiner**, etc., it will be replaced
with the one word **dessen; ihren, ihre**, etc. becomes
deren.

13.3.2. Put the relative pronoun at the head of the relative
clause, and the inflected verb at the end.

13.3.3. Insert the relative clause immediately after the noun
it refers to, unless the only word following that noun
in the main clause is an infinitive or a past participle.
The infinitive or past participle may then intervene
between the antecedent and the relative pronoun.
Examples:

    Das Bier ist ausgezeichnet. Man kann es in Karlsruhe kaufen.
    Das Bier, das man in Karlsruhe kaufen kann, ist ausgezeichnet.

    Paul wollte mir den Stein zeigen. Der Junge hatte ihn
    geworfen.
    Paul wollte mir den Stein zeigen, den der Junge geworfen
    hatte.

§14. *EXTENDED ADJECTIVE AND PARTICIPLE CONSTRUCTIONS*

14.1. In formal written German, which is more condensed than informal German, the writer can save words by piling modification upon modification, rather than using looser constructions. In informal German, relative clauses [§13] are
commonly used, whereas in formal German some of these are
replaced with extended participle constructions. Note the
following constructions.

14.1.1.   Informal: Eine Biene ist ein Insekt, das Honig liefert.
                Formal: Eine Biene ist ein Honig lieferndes Insekt.

The inflected verb of the relative clause liefert corresponds to the present participle lieferndes [§9.2.8].
This present participle has a double function: as a
verb form it can have a direct object: Honig; as an
adjective it has an ending to agree with das Insekt.

14.1.2.   Informal: Der Niederschlag ist die Feuchtigkeit, die aus
                           der Atmosphäre auf die Erde niederfällt.
                Formal: Der Niederschlag ist die aus der Atmosphäre
                           auf die Erde niederfallende Feuchtigkeit.

The inflected verb of the relative clause niederfällt
corresponds to the present participle niederfallende.
Both the inflected verb and the present participle are
modified by the two prepositional phrases: aus der
Atmosphäre and auf die Erde.

14.1.3.   Informal: Ein Stichwort ist ein Wort, das in einem Lexi-
                           kon behandelt ist.
                Formal: Ein Stichwort ist ein in einem Lexikon be-
                           handeltes Wort.

The relative clause may have a past participle used
with a form of sein as a predicate adjective. In the
extended construction the participle is used with its
appropriate adjective ending.

14.1.4.   Informal: Die Lösung eines Problems ist ein Ausweg, der
                           durch Nachdenken gefunden worden ist.
                Formal: Die Lösung eines Problems ist ein durch Nach-
                           denken gefundener Ausweg.

When the relative clause has a past participle used as
part of a passive verb phrase, the past participle, with
its appropriate adjective ending, is used in the extended
construction. The prepositional phrase of the relative
clause appears in the extended construction, but the
auxiliary verbs which form the passive verb phrase (here:
worden ist) are omitted. [§7.5.1; §10.3]

14.1.5.   Informal: Eine Institution ist eine Einrichtung, die für
                           bestimmte Aufgaben zuständig ist.
                Formal: Eine Institution ist eine für bestimmte Auf-
                           gaben zuständige Einrichtung.

When the relative clause has a predicate adjective with
a form of sein, that adjective, with its appropriate
adjective ending, is used in the extended construction.
An adjective, like a participle, may be modified by a
prepositional phrase. The prepositional phrase appears
in the extended construction, but the form of sein is
omitted.

14.1.6.   Informal: Die Ausgangsstoffe sind die Substanzen, die zu
                           verarbeiten sind.
                Formal: Die Ausgangsstoffe sind die zu verarbeitenden
                           Substanzen.

When the relative clause has a construction composed of
sein + **zu** + infinitive [see §7.5.3], this corresponds to
the construction **zu** + present participle [§9.2.8], which
has its appropriate adjective ending. The form of **sein**
is omitted in the extended construction.

Note: In English a translation of an extended adjective or
participle construction takes the form of a relative
clause; for example, the translation of both informal and
formal versions of §14.1.6 is: The raw materials are the
substances which are to be processed.

14.2. In order to understand formal German, the reader must de-
velop skill in recognizing the extended adjective construction. The clearest warning signal is a definite or indefinite article or a possessive adjective followed immediately
by a completely unrelated, unexpected word, for example, a
pronoun or a preposition. Combinations like: **ein uns, diese
sich, eine für, sein ohne** are signs to watch out for. Until
the learner becomes accustomed to this German construction,
he must first find the noun which matches the introductory
article or possessive adjective, and then work back to the
beginning. It is sometimes useful to make a relative clause
out of the extended adjective construction, as demonstrated
in §14.1.1-6. Further examples of extended adjective constructions:

> Eine Seuche ist _eine_ sich schnell ausbreitende, gefähr-
> liche, ansteckende <u>Krankheit</u>.

> Böll ist unter den Autoren, die literarisch zählen, <u>der</u> am
> weitesten verbreitete und am meisten übersetzte
> <u>Schriftsteller</u> in Europa.

> Wenn man heute von ‚deutscher Emigration' spricht, denkt man
> zunächst nicht an <u>die</u> unzähligen aus rassischen oder
> politischen Gründen zur Auswanderung <u>Gezwungenen</u>, son-
> dern an die Künstler, Universitätsprofessoren und Politiker...

The last example shows how a past participle used as an adjective can function as a noun (Gezwungenen) and still re-
tain the properties of an adjective, that is, the adjective
ending and modification by a prepositional phrase. [§2.6]

§15. _PRE/POSTPOSITIONS_

A preposition is a word used with a following noun or pronoun
to form a prepositional phrase. If, instead of preceding the
noun or pronoun in the phrase, this word follows it, it is called
a postposition. The postposition is a common occurrence in English as well as in German: all the way <u>through</u>; die ganze Nacht
über.
In both languages there are also phrases that have both a pre-
and a postposition: <u>from</u> now <u>on</u>; **von** nun **an**.
Learning difficulties arise when the idiomatic usages of pre-
and postposition do not correspond in the two languages. For
example: English: three months ago (postposition), German:

vor drei Monaten (preposition); along the street, die Straße
entlang.
In combination with a preposition, the postposition often indicates a direction: from the top down, from the ground up;
zum Fenster hinaus, durch den Wald hindurch. [Cf. also nach:
§18.6.2.]

§16. *COMPOUNDING OF NOUNS*

16.1. A speaker of German, like a speaker of English, can express new ideas by combining nouns in new ways. However,
the writer of German puts down his new combinations as
one string of letters, with no spaces and usually no
hyphens to indicate where one word ends and the next begins. Since many compound nouns are not listed in a dictionary, the reader must break them down into their component parts in order to recognize their meanings. There
are several characteristic ways to form compound nouns,
some of which involve a joining element.

16.1.1. noun + noun (+ noun...):
 das Möbel + der Wagen = der Möbelwagen - *furniture van*
 der Strumpf + die Hose = die Strumpfhose - *panty hose (but
  notice which part is the "panty" and which the "hose")*

16.1.2. noun + -s + noun:
 die Universität + -s + die Straße = die Universitätsstraße
 die Regierung + -s + die Form = die Regierungsform
 das Schlafen + -s + die Zeit = die Schlafenszeit

When an infinitive used as a noun [§2.5] or a noun ending in -tum, -ling, -heit, -keit, -schaft, -ung, -sion,
-tion, or -tät is combined with a following noun, the
joining element is regularly -s.

16.1.3. noun + -n + noun:
 die Tasche + -n + das Geld = das Taschengeld
 die Straße + -n + die Bahn = die Straßenbahn

16.1.4. noun - -e + noun:
 die Schule - -e + der Hof = der Schulhof - *school yard*
 die Kirche - -e + der Gang = der Kirchgang - *church-going*

There is no "rule" governing the combination of a noun
ending in -e with a following noun. Sometimes a joining
element -n is added (as in §16.1.3), sometimes the final
-e is dropped. Examples:
 die Kirche - -e + der Gänger = der Kirchgänger - *church-goer*
 die Kirche + -n + die Glocke = die Kirchenglocke - *church bell*

16.1.5. infinitive - -(e)n + noun:
 putzen - -en + die Frau = die Putzfrau - *cleaning woman*
 bauen - -en + das Holz = das Bauholz - *lumber*
 schneiden - -n + der Zahn = der Schneidezahn - *incisor*

16.1.6. adjective + noun:
 blau + die Säure = die Blausäure - *prussic acid*
 fein + der Schmecker = der Feinschmecker - *gourmet*
 schwarz + der Wald = der Schwarzwald - *Black Forest*

16.1.7. preposition / adverb + noun:

>   unter + der Gang = der Untergang - *decline*
>   ober + die Fläche = die Oberfläche - *surface*

Compounds can be formed in various combinations, for example:

>   die Sonne + -n + auf + der Gang = der Sonnenaufgang - *sunrise*

16.2. The gender of a compound noun is that of its last element:

>   der Wagen + die Pflege = die Wagenpflege - *car maintenance*
>   schreiben - -en + der Tisch = der Schreibtisch - *desk*

§17. *DA-/DAR- AND WO-/WOR-*

17.1. da-/dar- (The syllable **dar-** is used before a vowel.)
All the prepositions followed by the accusative or dative
(except **bis, ohne**) [§1.2.2-3; §1.3.3-4] can be combined
with the syllable **da-** or **dar-**: **daneben, dabei, dagegen;
daraus, darüber, darum.** The syllable **da-/dar-** is used in
place of a pronoun referring to a nonanimate object or to
a concept which may be represented by a clause or an infinitive phrase. It is not used to refer to a living being which has a proper name. This combination of **da-/dar-**
+ preposition is called a pronominal adverb. The pronominal adverb may be used to refer back to an element in the
same or a preceding sentence; it may also refer ahead to
an element following it within the same sentence.

17.1.1. In the following examples the pronominal adverb refers
back to a thing or concept in a preceding sentence or
part of the same sentence.

>   Vor dem Feuer steht ein Sessel, und darin liegt die Katze.
>   (darin = im Sessel)
>   Mein Mann wollte den alten Wagen verkaufen. Ich war dagegen.
>   (dagegen = gegen den Plan, den Wagen zu verkaufen)

17.1.2. If a sentence involves a verb followed by a preposition,
for example: **sprechen über, sich freuen über, sich erinnern an, warten auf, sich handeln um,** and the preposition has as its object an entire clause or an infinitive
phrase, then the pronominal adverb is used to link the
two parts of the sentence.

>   Wir warten darauf, daß er kommt. (da = daß er kommt)
>   *(We are waiting for him to come.)*
>
>   Ich weiß nichts davon, wieviel es ihm gekostet hat. (da =
>   wieviel es ihm gekostet hat)
>   *(I have no idea how much it cost him.)*
>
>   Wir haben darüber gesprochen, daß der Wirbelsturm viel
>   Schaden verursachte. (da- = daß der ...verursachte)
>   *(We talked about the fact that the tornado caused a great
>   deal of damage.)*

17.1.3. In addition to their use as pronominal adverbs which
clearly refer to an element either preceding or following them, some of these words are used idiomatically as
sentence adverbs or conjunctions with a specialized
meaning. The following may be especially tricky:

> dabei - *moreover, at the same time*   dafür - *instead*
> dagegen - *on the contrary, however*   damit [§18.3] - *so that*
> darauf - *thereupon, after that*   darum - *for this reason*
> darüber hinaus - *besides, in addition*
> dazu - *for this reason, for this purpose; in addition*

17.2. wo-/wor- (The syllable **wor-**, like **dar-**, is used before a vowel.)

Parallel to the pronominal adverbs with **da-/dar-** discussed above, **wo-** and **wor-** can be combined with prepositions: **wobei, wogegen; woraus, worin.** These compounds function as interrogative or relative pronominal adverbs.

17.2.1. As interrogatives, these pronominal adverbs are equivalent to preposition + **was.**

> Woran denkst du?   Worum handelt es sich?
> Worin besteht der Unterschied zwischen „Schreibtisch" und „Pult"?

17.2.2. As relatives, these pronominal adverbs are equivalent to preposition + a relative pronoun which refers to something non-animate or to a whole concept. When **wo-/wor-** + preposition is used as a relative, it usually refers to a whole concept.

> Der Sohn wollte Flieger werden, womit seine Mutter gar nicht einverstanden war. (wo- = der Sohn wollte Flieger werden)

§18. *SOME WORDS WITH VARIOUS GRAMMATICAL FUNCTIONS*

18.1. als

The word **als** is a function word which has many idiomatic usages, each corresponding to a different idiom in English. The most frequent of these usages are:

18.1.1. As a subordinating conjunction which indicates that the time period expressed in the subordinate clause is the same as the time period of the main clause: "when, as, while." [See also §8.4.1.1.1.]

> Gerade als ich gehen wollte, klingelte das Telephon.

18.1.2. As part of the expressions **als ob, als wenn,** which function as subordinating conjunctions: "as if, as though."

> Er tat, als ob er nicht gehen wollte. *(He acted as though he didn't want to leave.)*

When the full phrase is expressed, this usage presents no difficulty. However, **ob** or **wenn** may be omitted, in which case the inflected verb immediately follows **als.** [See also §11.5.]

> Er tat, als wollte er nicht gehen.

The position of the inflected verb unmistakably differentiates the first usage from the second, that is:

> als .... verb - when / als verb .... - as if.

18.1.3. Following a comparative [§4.8.1] or **ander-**: **größer als** - bigger than; **anders als** - different from, other than.

18.1.4. Following **nichts, niemand: nichts als** – nothing but, nothing except.

18.1.5. As an indication of a characteristic, in connection with a noun or adjective.

> Als mein Freund hat er mir geraten, es nicht zu tun. *(As my friend, he advised me not to do it.)*

> Die Nachricht hat sich als falsch herausgestellt. *(The news report turned out to be false.)*

18.1.6. In the idiomatic expression **zu** + adjective, **als daß.**

> Frau Hahn war zu müde, als daß sie weiter arbeiten konnte. *(Mrs. Hahn was too tired to continue working.)*

18.1.7. In the expression **sowohl...als (auch)** – both...and..., ...as well as..., not only...but also...

> sowohl Männer als auch Frauen *(both men and women, not only men but also women, men as well as women)*

18.2. da

The word **da** has two main functions:

18.2.1. The subordinating conjunction **da** – since, because, in view of the fact that. This conjunction is unmistakably identified by the fact that it is the first word in a subordinate clause, in which the inflected verb is at the end [§8.4.1]

> Da die Frau stattlich war und sehr tüchtig, stellten sich Freier ein. *(Because the woman was handsome and very capable, suitors presented themselves.)*

Note: Sometimes in older texts, or in modern texts in which old-fashioned language is being imitated, the subordinating conjunction **da** is used with an expression of time to mean "when."

> Und er machte sich auf und kam zu seinem Vater. Da er aber noch ferne von dannen war, sah ihn sein Vater,... *(And he arose, and came to his father. But when he was yet a great way off, his father saw him,...)* — Luke 15, 20

18.2.2. The adverb **da** – there, then, at that place, at that time. This adverb appears in independent and in subordinate clauses; it has no correlation with the position of the inflected verb.

> Eines Tages saß er bei ihr in der Stube, und da kam ihr der Gedanke,... *(One day he sat with her in her parlor, and at that time the thought came to her...)*

18.3. damit

The word **damit** has two functions:

18.3.1. The subordinating conjunction **damit** – so that, in order that. This conjunction is unmistakably identified by the fact that it is the first word in a subordinate clause, in which the inflected verb is at the end.

Man riet ihr zu, sich einen neuen Mann zu nehmen, damit ihre
Einsamkeit ein Ende habe. *(People advised her to take a new
husband, so that her loneliness might come to an end.)*

Morgens und abends fuhr er einen Umweg, nur damit ich nicht
mit der Straßenbahn fahren mußte. *(Mornings and evenings he
drove a roundabout way just so that I didn't have to take the
streetcar.)*

Note that in the first example above, **damit** is followed
by a subjunctive form, in the second by an indicative.

18.3.2. The pronominal adverb **damit** [§17.1.] - with it, with
them, with that, with those, with the fact that. This
adverb appears in independent and subordinate clauses;
it has no correlation with the position of the inflected
verb.

Er nahm die Taschenlampe und leuchtete damit unter den Tisch.
(damit = mit der Taschenlampe [§17.1.1])

Man muß immer damit rechnen, daß es in Deutschland viel regnet.
(da- = daß es in Deutschland viel regnet [§17.1.2])

Note: The conjunction **damit** is always stressed on the
second syllable; the adverb may be stressed on either,
according to meaning.

18.4. ein

18.4.1. By far the most frequent usage of **ein** is as the indefinite article, with the case endings given in §4.3.

In einem Dorf lebte eine brave Ehefrau...

18.4.2. The word **ein** is also the numeral "one." As such it is
often used with the definite article: **der eine, das
eine, die einen,** etc.

Die Frau bot alles auf, um ihren Mann aufzufinden, denn sie
hatte ja nur den einen. *(The woman made every effort to lo-
cate her husband, for she had, after all, only the one.)*

18.4.3. Occasionally **einen** or **einem** stands alone; **einen** is
then the accusative of **man,** and **einem** is the dative.
[§5.5.1]

Das erinnert einen an Zeiten, wo man glücklicher war.

Wenn einem nicht wohl ist, bleibt man besser zu Hause.

18.4.4. When **ein** (a stressed form of the preposition **in**) is at
the end of a clause, it is the separable part of a compound verb, as in §9.5.1. An appropriate meaning for
the verb is to be found only by looking up the infinitive of the complete compound.

Freier stellten sich ein, die der Frau die Ehe antrugen.
(sich ein·stellen - *appear, show up*)

18.5. lassen

18.5.1. As an independent verb, **lassen** means: leave, let have;
stop, leave off.

Rumpelstilzchen ließ der Königin ihr Kind.

Laß das! *(Stop that!)*

Mein Neffe kann das Rauchen nicht lassen. *(My nephew can't stop smoking.)*

18.5.2. Person as subject + **lassen** + (sich) + infinitive may have the meaning of permitting someone to do something or causing something to be done.

Example of permission:
Lassen Sie die alten Leute ihre Wohnung behalten! *(Let the old people keep their house!)*

Examples of cause:
Zunächst ließ Herr Schwerdtlein den Arzt rufen. *(First of all Mr. Schwerdtlein had the doctor called.)*

Der Kaiser will sich Kleider aus dem magischen Stoff machen lassen. *(The emperor wants to have clothes made [for himself] out of the magic material.)*

18.5.3. Inanimate thing as subject + **lassen** sich + infinitive has a passive meaning [§7.5.2]

Dieser Stoff läßt sich leicht verarbeiten. *(This material can be easily processed.)*

18.6. nach [may be either a preposition or a postposition: §15]

18.6.1. As a preposition + dative [§1.3.3]:
18.6.1.1. With a time word as its object, **nach** - after:
nach zwei Jahren; nach einer Zeitlang; Viertel nach elf.
18.6.1.2. With a place word as object, **nach** - toward, to:
nach Europa; nach Stuttgart; nach außen hin; nach oben.

18.6.2. As a preposition + dative or postposition preceded by dative, with objects other than place or time words, for example, the name of a person or something referring to an opinion or a statement, **nach** - according to:
meiner Meinung nach; nach dieser Theorie.
Ich kenne ihn nur dem Namen nach. *(I know him only by name.)*

18.7. um
The word um has several functions which correspond to different idiomatic expressions in English. The most frequent usages are:

18.7.1. As a preposition + accusative indicating a spatial relationship:
um die Ecke *(around the corner)*

18.7.2. As a preposition + accusative indicating a temporal relationship:
um acht Uhr *(at eight o'clock)*
Note: *around eight o'clock* - gegen acht Uhr

18.7.3. As a preposition + accusative indicating the amount of difference in measurement of time, space, and the like:

Sie war um ein Jahr älter als er. *(She was a year older than he.)*

18.7.4. As a preposition + accusative used with certain verbs or adjectives:

> bitten um – *ask for;* es geht um – *the problem is;*
> es handelt sich um – *the question is, it is a question of;*
> sich kümmern um – *care about, concern oneself with;*
> es ist schade um – *it's too bad about*

18.7.5. In the expression um...zu – to, in order to. <u>Caution:</u> Remember that **zu** occurs between the separable part of the verb and the stem: auszusehen, einzuladen, mitzu-machen.

> um schnell einzuschlafen – *in order to fall asleep quickly*

18.7.6. In the expression um so (= desto) + comparative:

> um so besser – *all the better, so much the better*

18.7.7. As the separable part of a two-part verb, occurring at the end of a clause:

> um·sehen – *look around;* um·bringen – *kill;* um·kommen – *perish*

18.8. zwar

18.8.1. **und zwar:** When **zwar** is preceded by **und,** more precise information is to be expected.

> Herr Kayser fährt doch nach Hause, und zwar in ein paar Tagen. *(Mr. Kayser <u>is</u> going home, and he's going to do it within a few days.)*

18.8.2. **zwar...aber:** When **zwar** is at the beginning or in the middle of a clause, the conjunction **aber** is to be expected. The information following **aber** expresses a restriction or limitation of the previous statement.

> Ihr Wagen ist zwar gut gepflegt, aber er hat einige Rostflek-ken. [§19.2.1] *(Your car is in good repair, it is true, but it has some rust spots.)*

§19. *SOME FEATURES OF GERMAN PRINTING*

19.1. -ß-/-ss-

The spellings -ß- and -ss- represent the same sound — the one in "hiss" in English. The letter -ß- is used:

19.1.1. at the end of a word: ließ, Fluß, Fuß;

19.1.2. before another consonant: du ißt, er läßt, ihr müßt, ich wußte, bißchen, häßlich, einflußlos, seßhaft;

19.1.3. between vowels if the preceding vowel is long: Füße, stoßen.

Note: Within a word, the use of -ss- between vowels indicates that the preceding vowel is short: Gasse, Flüs-se, passieren, müssen, geschlossen; -ß- indicates that the preceding vowel is long: Straße, Füße, gestoßen — a diphthong is equivalent to a long vowel: schmeißen, draußen, Äußerung.

19.2. Special usages of hyphens

19.2.1. A hyphen is used to "break" a word if part of the word is at the end of a line of print and the rest of the word is at the beginning of the next line. For such breaks, the letter **-ß-** between two vowels is always put with the latter part of the word, at the beginning of the second line. Examples: **hei-ßen, drau-ßen, schlie-ßen.**

The combination **-ck-** is broken into **k-k** and divided between the first and second parts of the word: **Stük-ke, Zuk-ker.**

Note: The same usages are followed in printing the words in a musical text.

19.2.2. Whenever combinations of two or more compounds have a shared element, a hyphen is used: **Land-, Forst- und Wasserwirtschaft = Landwirtschaft, Forstwirtschaft und Wasserwirtschaft.**

19.3. Punctuation with numerals

19.3.1. Ordinals are indicated by a period after the numeral:

> im 19. Jahrhundert = im neunzehnten Jahrhundert
> den 15. April = den fünfzehnten April
> Friedrich II. = Friedrich der Zweite
> von Ludwig XIV. = von Ludwig dem Vierzehnten

19.3.2. The decimal is indicated by a comma:

> 0,47 = Null Komma siebenundvierzig

19.3.3. Trios of digits in large numerals are set off by a space:

> 1 376 455 = eine Million dreihundertsechsundsiebzigtausend vierhundertfünfundfünfzig

or by a period:

> Österreich hat eine Bevölkerung von 7.073.800 Personen.

19.4. Spaced printing: Emphasis on a word is indicated by so-called "S p e r r d r u c k."